OUT OF EVERY
TRIBE AND
NATION

OUT OF EVERY TRIBE AND NATION

Christian Theology at the Ethnic Roundtable

JUSTO L. GONZÁLEZ

ABINGDON PRESS
Nashville

OUT OF EVERY TRIBE AND NATION:
CHRISTIAN THEOLOGY AT THE ETHNIC ROUNDTABLE

Library of Congress Cataloging-in-Publication Data
González, Justo L.
   Out of every tribe and nation : Christian theology at the ethnic roundtable / Justo L. González.
      p.   cm.
   Includes bibliographical references.
   ISBN 0-687-29860-1 (pbk.)
   1. Theology, Doctrinal.   2. Christianity and culture.
3. Intercultural communication.   I. Title.
BT78.G637   1992
230'.089—dc20   92-15159
                                                                         CIP

Scripture quotations, except for brief paraphrases or unless otherwise noted, are from the New Revised Standard Version Bible, copyright © 1989, by the Division of Christian Education of the National Council of the Churches of Christ in the United States of America and are used by permission.

MANUFACTURED IN THE UNITED STATES OF AMERICA

CONTENTS

Contents

ACKNOWLEDGMENTS

This book is the result of several years of dialogue. Although that dialogue has included a wide variety of persons from different parts of the world—and even, through their writings, many others long dead—it has most actively involved the participants of the United Methodist Roundtable of Ethnic Minority Theologians, sponsored by the Division of Ordained Ministry of the Board of Higher Education and Ministry. This group, meeting regularly since 1987, has been a lively and friendly forum for the discussion of the topics addressed in the pages that follow, and it is to them that I owe most of the ideas expressed therein. In particular, I am grateful for the graciousness and seriousness with which the Roundtable devoted its 1991 session to a discussion of a preliminary draft of this book, thus adding many an insight and preventing many a pitfall.

The Roundtable has been composed of United Methodists, with an occasional observer from another denomination. This is a testimonial to the commitment of The United Methodist Church to pluralism. Also, the very fact that we felt free to criticize rather harshly much of what our denomination has done and is doing vis-à-vis ethnic minorities is a sign of openness in United Methodism which we celebrate. At the same time, although most of us speaking around the Roundtable were United Methodists, we were very much aware of the church catholic, and as we offer the results of our deliberations we do so in the hope that they will prove useful, not only for United Methodism, but also to the rest of the church.

Among the participants in the Roundtable, I wish to record my special thanks to those who have served consecutively as its administrative staff, Young Joon Cho and KilSang Yoon, and to their support staff, Ms. Lynn Strother Hinkle.

Among the friends and colleagues outside the Roundtable who have read portions of this manuscript, or who have commented on them as I have made oral presentations of their contents, none has been as supportive or as helpful as my wife, Dr. Catherine Gunsalus González, Professor of Church History at Columbia Theological Seminary.

But above all, I must express my gratitude to the worldwide communion of the Church of Jesus Christ, particularly that portion of it which calls itself United Methodist. I often lose patience with it, only to be reminded once and again that, by the grace of God, it has had far more patience with me than I deserve!

THE ROUNDTABLE

PARTICIPANTS

William Sione 'Amanake Havea
  Tonga
Marvin B. Abrams
  La Mirada, Calif.
Bilha Alegría
  Oakland, Calif.
Albert J. D. Aymer
  Madison, N.J.
María Luisa Santillán Baert
  Nashville, Tenn.
Roy D. Barton
  Dallas, Tex.
John H. Cartwright
  Boston, Mass.
Ignacio Castuera
  Hollywood, Calif.
Young Joon Cho
  Hamden, Conn.
Young-Ho Chun
  Kansas City, Mo.
Karen Collier
  Nashville, Tenn.
Leo M. Constantino
  Wheaton, Ill.
Patricia Dumont Davidson
  Chiloquin, Oreg.
Cain H. Felder
  Washington, D.C.

Douglass E. Fitch
  Pasadena, Calif.
Finees Flores
  San Antonio, Tex.
Benjamin T. Fong
  San Francisco, Calif.
Justo L. González
  Decatur, Ga.
S. Michael Hahm
  New York, N.Y.
David Junichi Harada
  Torrance, Calif.
Ramón Hernández
  Ponce, P.R.
Sue Ellen Herne
  Hogansburg, N.Y.
Zan Holmes
  Dallas, Tex.
Hidemi Ito
  Los Angeles, Calif.
Chan Hie Kim
  Claremont, Calif.
Stephen S. Kim
  Claremont, Calif.
Lydia Lebrón-Rivera
  Jersey City, N.J.
Jung Young Lee
  Madison, N.J.

9

David Long, Jr.
Dewey, Okla.
Ediberto López
New York, N.Y.
William B. McClain
Washington, D.C.
David Maldonado, Jr.
Dallas, Tex.
James J. M. Misajon
Honolulu, Hawaii
Jay Hyon Nahm
Shaker Heights, Okla.
Homer Noley
Oklahoma City, Okla.
Tevita T. Puloka
San Mateo, Calif.
Daniel R. Rodríguez-Díaz
Chicago, Ill.
Cornish R. Rogers
Claremont, Calif.
Kyung-Lim Shin-Lee
Washington, D.C.
James J. M. Shropshire
Washington, D.C.
Tweedy Evelene Sombrero
Phoenix, Ariz.
Naomi Southard
Oakland, Calif.
Timothy Ting
Alhambra, Calif.
William C. Turner, Jr.
Durham, N.C.
Vivencio L. Vinluan
South Gate, Calif.
Lloyd K. Wake
San Francisco, Calif.
Henry Wilkins IV
Dallas, Tex.
Tallulah F. Williams
Chicago, Ill.
Edward P. Wimberly
Evanston, Ill.
Sam Wynn
Fayetteville, N.C.

KaoFang Yeh
La Verne, Calif.
KilSang Yoon
Nashville, Tenn.
Henry James Young
Evanston, Ill.

OBSERVERS

Joseph V. Crockett
Nashville, Tenn.
Ernest T. Dixon
San Antonio, Tex.
Jacquelyn Grant
Atlanta, Ga.
C. Jarrett Gray, Jr.
Meadville, Pa.
Lynn Strother Hinkle
Nashville, Tenn.
Arturo Mariscal
San Antonio, Tex.
Peter Nash
Evanston, Ill.
Arthur Pressley
Madison, N.J.
Keith Rae
New York, N.Y.
Marcia Y. Riggs
Decatur, Ga.
Michael G. Rivas
New York, N.Y.
Esdras Rodríguez-Díaz
Washington, D.C.
Thomas W. Spann
Dallas, Tex.
Hidetoshi Tanaka
Washington, D.C.
Marion Wake
San Francisco, Calif.
Daryl Ward
Dayton, Ohio
Richard Yaeger
Nashville, Tenn.

OUT OF EVERY
TRIBE AND
NATION

CHAPTER ONE

INTRODUCTION

This book is a celebration of discovery. For four years, a group of ethnic minority theologians have been gathering in a "Roundtable." We have had some lively and exciting theological discussions, and all of us have had experiences of theological discovery. But above all, we have discovered one another. In a sweatlodge in Arizona, to the accompaniment of mariachis in San Antonio, in a Korean church in Chicago, and to the beat of ancient spirituals on St. Helena Island, we have come to understand one another's hopes and pains, as well as the faith we live by. As John H. Cartwright put it, "Something happened to all of us." That is the discovery this book celebrates, and the discovery to which it also invites its readers.

As this book goes to press, people on both sides of the Atlantic are preparing to celebrate the quincentennial of the so-called discovery of America. Such celebration, and even the very word "discovery," are signs of a blindly ethnocentric world view. If to discover means to find something hitherto unknown, Columbus discovered nothing, for the lands that he supposedly discovered had been known and inhabited for thousands of years. Columbus, in fact, was lost, for he had sailed on the basis of a gross miscalculation of the earth's circumference. When he arrived at these shores, he had no idea where he was. And when he returned to Spain, he had no idea where he had been. Was this a great feat of navigation, worthy of celebration five hundred years later?

There was indeed the opportunity for discovery. Europe could have discovered how parochial its own world view was. It could have discovered its own limited place within the span of humankind. Certainly, the native inhabitants of these lands soon were forced to discover the overwhelming military power and greed of the European invaders. But all that Europe really discovered was that there were others whom it could conquer and exploit by guile and deceit. The descendants of the Germanic tribes that invaded the Roman Empire had long found their further advance to the south and to the east blocked by more powerful Moslem neighbors. But now, far to the west, across the ocean, there was a realm inhabited by people to be looted and robbed of life, liberty, and land—in many cases, people whose own spirit of hospitality made them even more vulnerable. That was the great European discovery five hundred years ago. It was a discovery whose consequences can still be seen throughout the world, but hardly one worthy of celebration!

Some who are slightly more enlightened suggest that, instead of speaking of a "discovery," we should speak of an "encounter of two cultures." Encounter indeed! An encounter like a head-on collision between an eighteen-wheeler and a bicycle! There was little mutuality in that encounter. True, Europe learned much from it, so that today it is difficult to imagine Ireland without potatoes, or Italy without tomatoes. But, given the enormous disparity in military power, there was no mutuality in the encounter. The native inhabitants of these lands were not even allowed to name themselves. Columbus had sailed for India, and therefore they were Indians. (A Native American has commented that he is glad Columbus was not looking for Turkey!)[1] Robbed of a name, the "Indians" were soon robbed also of their land, their freedom, and their traditions. And let us not deceive ourselves into thinking that this was done only by the Spanish. It was done by the Spanish, by the Portuguese, by the English, and by almost every immigrant whose descendants now hold land anywhere from Alaska to Tierra del Fuego.

What took place five hundred years ago was the beginning of a vast Western expansion and domination. What Columbus and those who followed him did in the Americas, Magellan and those who came after him did in the Pacific.[2] Slaves were brought from Africa to the Americas in order to cultivate lands that had been taken from the natives—a clear example of how one oppression leads to another. The westward expansion of the United States, so celebrated by the national mythology, was in reality a cruel and greedy land-grab, at the cost of much suffering and many thousands of lives among the original inhabitants of the land. Mexico was provoked to war and then crushed and humiliated on the basis of a supposedly "manifest destiny" of the nation. Around the globe, the British, Dutch, French, and others imitated what Spain and Portugal had done in the Americas. In all of this, there was much suffering and oppression, some who became extremely rich and many who were robbed of their meager possessions; but there was no mutual discovery. The conquered had to learn about their conquerors for sheer survival; but he conquerors only needed to know how to control and exploit the conquered.

Now, five hundred years later, is it too late to undertake a new and real discovery—a true encounter among people of different races and differ-

ent cultural backgrounds? It certainly would seem so, as we engage in bois-
terous and mindless celebrations of the quincentennial of that earlier
false "discovery." It certainly would seem so, for now we have to deal, not
only with the mutual discovery of Native Americans and European immigrants, but also with that mixed breed of both Native American and European descent whom we call "Hispanics," and with the descendants of the
African immigrants brought here against their will, and with Asian Americans, Pacific Islanders, and with a host of others whom society at large
prefers to ignore rather than to discover.

There are powerful forces arrayed against such a discovery. There
are the forces of inertia, parochialism, and racism, which push people
in our society to stay among others "of their own kind." And there are
the forces of self-interest, for a true discovery would force us to deal
more justly with one another—unlike the European invaders, who justified taking the lands of the Native Americans by dubbing them "savages."

Yet it is precisely to such discovery that God is calling the church today.
It will not be an easy task, for it goes against the grain of our imbedded
cultural racism, against many of our own self-interests, and against much
of the current political trend. But God has never called the church to easy
tasks. Tasks that can be undertaken without an overpowering faith-
command might as well be left to others. It is the tasks that the world
deems impossible that most appropriately belong to the church. If so, the
task of promoting a new and true mutual discovery among the peoples of
this earth is certainly the task of the church.

The Roundtable of Ethnic Theologians hopes to make its contribution,
however small, to that task. Those who organized it were convinced that,
if the church is to make a dent in the racism and tribalism that permeate
life in the United States—and in the world at large—it has to begin by
promoting among its own members the sort of encounter and mutual discovery that did not take place five hundred years ago.

The Roundtable is one of many ways to promote such an encounter.
Beginning in 1987, and every year since that date, ethnic minority theologians have been gathering as a group "to look at the various loci of
traditional theology from their own perspectives, and to enter into dialogue with each other and with traditional theology, seeking a better
and deeper understanding of the gospel of Jesus Christ."[3] The group,
usually about twenty, includes Native Americans, Hispanics, African
Americans, and Asian Americans, with representation from various sub-
groups within these larger groups. They are men and women, laity and
clergy, pastors and professors, with the common denominator of a deep
commitment to the Christian faith as well as to their own cultures and
traditions.

According to our various experiences, we have brought different concerns and contributions to the Roundtable. Native Americans have expressed their pain at being robbed of their land, and now seeing that land, sacred to their ancient traditions, violated and destroyed. African Americans have given us a glimpse of the pain of slavery, and of the frustration of having built the wealth of a nation, only to be denied the fruits of that wealth. Hispanic and Asian Americans have expressed the tensions and the joys of biculturalism and bilingualism, the generational conflicts they produce, and the questions of identity they pose. Others of us have brought concerns having to do with other forms of oppression operating both in society at large and in our own ethnic groups. In this respect, feminist and womanist theologies have made an important contribution to our discussion. Yet such a summary of the concerns that each has brought to the Roundtable fails to do justice to the intensity, the pain, and the joy of our encounter. Something happens deep in the soul when, after a long day of intense theological debate, all sit around a fire in a sweatlodge, expressing hopes and dreams not often voiced, and each concluding with the phrase, "all my relatives." Hope and anger mix and boil when, on an island off the Carolina coast, one finds a stable and peaceful community, built by the descendants of the slaves who also built the ancient plantations, now being threatened by outside "developers."

The task of the Roundtable has been defined sharply.[4] Our purpose is to learn from one another, as we jointly look at the theology that has been taught and bequeathed to us, and to seek to correct it and to enrich it from the standpoint of our own ethnic and cultural backgrounds and experience. We have also sought to strengthen one another, for we are acutely aware that the reason why a true encounter was not possible at the time of the so-called discovery was the unequal power between the parties involved, and the invaders' knack of pitting one nation against another.[5] Likewise, if we are to make a contribution the church at large will heed and receive, we must make it in partnership with one another.

Concretely, the Roundtable has proceeded by having some of its members prepare papers on particular theological themes from the perspective of their own ethnic and cultural experience—we have had time to deal with hermeneutics, creation, salvation, and ecclesiology—and then calling for responses and general discussions.[6]

Although the discussions were often critical of traditional theology, and of the way the white establishment, both in church and in society at large, has used that theology to oppress or to ignore minorities, that was not the main topic of discussion, nor the mood of the meetings. A white observer who is keenly aware of the all-pervasive character of racism, reported:

This theological roundtable was different. Rarely was the emphasis placed on my sin (whites corporately). Rather, the conversation this time centered on what experiences and ideas each of the ethnic representatives had . . . that shape both their present faith and future possibilities for their faith as well as for that of the whole church. Occasionally the emphasis shifted to the oppression of whiteness, but most of the time this group was free of the normal "againstness" that I experience even when I am the only white person present when an oppressed group meets. I am not complaining about the frequent need for the call for repentance of whites, but I am celebrating the positive stance that this encounter took.[7]

From the beginning, it was planned that by 1992 a book would be written coming out of the experience of the Roundtable, yet "not as a compilation of papers and responses, but as a coherent whole in which the essence and results of our dialogue are expounded in such a way that readers can join in it."[8] This book attempts to be that "coherent whole." In the pages that follow I have sought to express much of what I have heard my colleagues say during these four years. I trust that I have been faithful to them, although I am acutely aware that it is impossible to convey in a document such as this the many learnings, theological as well as personal, that have taken place in our gatherings. Thus, after four years of deliberation, I would still insist on what I said at the conclusion of our first meeting:

More than all the things that have taken place here, more than all the things we have said, more than all the experiences we have shared, the most important point is that we have met, that we have really met, and that out of our meeting a new vision and a new dream have emerged. May that vision never fade. May that dream come true.[9]

At the threshold of the quincentennial of the so-called discovery, we have made a much more important and real discovery: We have discovered one another, and in this mutual discovery we have all been enriched. It is our hope that this book will help others meet with us, truly meet with us, so that we may discover one another, and jointly experience and express the true and full oneness which is in Christ.

As to the organization of the book itself, in the next chapter I shall discuss some of the presuppositions that I bring to the task of devising ethnic minority theologies, and which some others in the Roundtable share with me. Then, chapters 3 to 6 deal with each of the principal themes that have occupied the Roundtable, in the same order in which the Roundtable discussed them: first hermeneutics (chapter 3), followed by creation (chapter 4), then the doctrine of salvation (chapter 5), and finally ecclesiology (chapter 6). Quite clearly, this is just a selection of the many themes that could have been discussed. It is hoped, however, that this selection will suffice to give a glimpse into the gifts the church may receive as it opens itself to theological insights "out of every tribe and nation."

CHAPTER TWO

A VISION OF CATHOLICITY

What can possibly be the contribution of a "Roundtable of Ethnic Theologians"? Is not the Christian faith only one, the same for all people, in all places and circumstances? If so, what justification is there for theology arising out of various ethnic perspectives and experiences? Will this not further divide a church that, if anything, is in need of greater unity?

Perhaps the answer to these questions is to be found in Scripture itself—in the variety of witnesses and perspectives it encompasses within its canon.

THE FOURFOLD WITNESS TO THE GOSPEL

Why does the New Testament include four different gospels? Wouldn't it be much simpler to have a single gospel, one bringing together all the teachings to be found in our present four? It would certainly save us much irritation, as I found when as a high school student I sought to convert my classmates. Silvino, who had read some of the works of the Enlightenment, was quick to point out that the two genealogies in Matthew and Luke do not agree. On a particular occasion, when I had around me a group of attentive students listening to my testimony, he left me wordless by simply reading the various gospel accounts of the feeding of the multitude, and then asking how many times Jesus fed how many, with how many fishes and how many loaves. Others in my class were more receptive, but their questions were no less baffling. Marisol, whose parents were divorced, asked why in one gospel divorce is absolutely forbidden, and in another an exception is made. And Juan José, perhaps at the instigation of Silvino, wanted to know if Jesus had said "blessed are the poor," or "blessed are the poor in spirit."

I was very excited when I found among my father's books an old harmony of the gospels. Now I would be able to put them all together into a single coherent story, with no contradictions and no gaps! But I soon found out that the so-called harmony did not harmonize anything. On the contrary, it made the contrasts and the contradictions even more glaring. Where was Jesus born? How many years did he spend in his ministry? What was the order of events during that ministry? What did he actually say from the cross? Who were the first witnesses to his resurrection? The "harmony" simply served to show more clearly than ever that the gospels do not agree on these as well as on many other matters.

Why, then, did the early church decide to include four *different* gospels in its canon, thus subjecting later generations, not only to puzzlement, but also to the ridicule of any who would take the time to see the contradictions between these four accounts? Was it that they were not aware of the differences among the four?

The truth is that the early church included these four gospels in the canon *precisely because they were different.* In the struggle against various Gnostic interpretations of Christianity, which denied some of the crucial historical events of the life of Jesus, there was strength in the argument that these four witnesses, while differing in detail, agreed on the crucial matters under attack. In a court of law, it is difficult to impugn the testimony of a multiplicity of witnesses who, while differing in matters of detail, agree on the basic issue at hand. Indeed, if they agree in every detail their authority is questioned, for there is the likelihood that their testimony has been prearranged. Likewise, in the debates of the second century, the church found support for its insistence on the historical events of the life of Jesus, and for its rejection of Gnostic speculations, precisely in this multiform witness of the four gospels.

The most explicit passage from ancient times defending the use of four gospels comes from Irenaeus, who was bishop of Lyon late in the second century. Its importance is such that it is worthy of extensive quotation:

> It is not possible that the Gospels can be either more or fewer in number than they are. For, since there are four zones of the world in which we live, and four principal winds, while the Church is scattered throughout all the world, and the "pillar and ground" of the Church is the Gospel and the spirit of life; it is fitting that she should have four pillars, breathing out immortality on every side, and vivifying men afresh. From which fact, it is evident that the Word, the Artificer of all, He that sitteth upon the cherubim, and contains all things, He who was manifested to men, has given us the Gospel under four aspects, but bound together by one Spirit. . . . For this reason were four principal covenants given to the human race: one, prior to the deluge, under Adam; the second, that after the deluge, under Noah; the third, the giving of the law, under Moses; the fourth, that which renovates man, and sums up all things in itself by means of the Gospel, raising and bearing men upon its wings into the heavenly kingdom.

These things being so, all who destroy the form of the Gospel are vain, unlearned, and also audacious; those, [I mean,] who represent the aspects of the Gospel as being either more in number than as aforesaid, or, on the other hand, fewer. The former class [do so], that they may seem to have discovered more than is of the truth; the latter, that they may set the dispensations of God aside. . . . But that these Gospels alone are true and reliable, and admit neither an increase nor diminution of the aforesaid number, I have proved by so many and such [arguments]. For, since God made all things in due proportion and adaptation, it was fit also that the outward aspect of the Gospel should be well arranged and harmonized.[1]

Modern scholars have often ridiculed this passage, as if Irenaeus were building his argument on some magical connection based on the number four. Yet, there is much more to this passage. What Irenaeus is saying is not that, because there are four of this and four of that, there should also be four gospels. What he is saying is rather that the witnesses to the gospel must represent the entire *oikoumene*—the entire inhabited earth. In this *oikoumene*, there are four zones, and there are four "principal" or universal (the word he uses is "catholic") winds. Furthermore, this fourfold division of the *oikoumene* is not only geographical, but also chronological, for there are four "principal" or universal (again, "catholic") covenants throughout history. It is this universality of the gospel, this catholicity of the faith, that requires the fourfold witness of the four gospels. This fourfold witness is part of its wholeness, its catholicity.

At this point it may be helpful to make a slight detour in our argument, and discuss very briefly the original meaning of the term "catholic" as applied to the church and to its faith. The earliest extant Christian writer to use the expression "catholic church" was Ignatius of Antioch, who declared that, wherever Jesus Christ is, there is the "catholic church."[2] It has been argued[3] that Ignatius is using the term "catholic" in the sense of "universal," or "general," as it had been used by others long before,[4] and that it was only later that it came to mean the opposite of "heretical" or "sectarian."[5] Such an interpretation, however, does not take into account the context in which Ignatius uses the expression in question. He is attacking some who "care nothing about love," and who withdraw from the eucharistic celebration of the church. In response to such attitudes, he counsels the Smyrneans to flee from all division *(merismós)* as the root of evil. On the contrary, all are to be where the bishop is, just as the entire "*catholic* church" is present wherever Jesus is.

Thus, the phrase in question appears in a passage where Ignatius is stressing the opposition between orthodoxy and heresy. It is as part of that argument that he uses the term "catholic," whose etymological meaning is "according to the whole," in contrast to *merismós*, division. The difference between what Ignatius teaches and what his opponents hold is that his doctrines are "catholic," they are according to the whole, whereas theirs are partial, opinions held by a particular group which then raises them to the category of the universal. In other words, heretics err, among other things, because they do not pay heed to the entire "catholic" witness of the entire "catholic" church.

Slightly more than half a century after Ignatius, in the passage already quoted at length, Irenaeus is arguing that the catholicity of the church, that completeness which is an essential criterion of orthodoxy, requires the multiple witness of the four gospels. Indeed, those whom Irenaeus rejects as heretics are those "who represent the aspects of the Gospel as being either more in number than as aforesaid, or, on the other hand, fewer." Those who add new gospels of their own do so in order "that they may seem to have discovered more than is of the truth." In other words, they are innovators who wish to stand out as such. Among those who wish to have fewer than four gospels, Irenaeus mentions the Marcionites, who use only a mutilated version of Luke, and the Montanists and Encratites, who reject the Fourth Gospel. Among those who add a new gospel, he mentions the Valentinians, whose "Gospel of truth" must be rejected because it denies the truth of the other four gospels.[6]

The main point, however, is double: On the one hand, the multiform nature of the gospel is to be preserved by the admission of the four canonical gospels. On the other, no more gospels are to be admitted, as if any innovator such as Valentinus had the liberty to create an entirely new version of the gospel. This is the original meaning of catholicity, of true universality, of being "according to the whole." Unfortunately, today when we speak of "universality" we tend to speak in terms of uniformity: something is "universal" because it can be applied equally anywhere. In this sense, "universality" becomes the opposite of "catholic"—"according to the whole"—which includes a diverse totality.

There is both a closure and an openness to such catholicity. The closure is evident, and eventually became the dominant element in the understanding of catholicity. People are not free to invent new doctrines as they see fit. What made this evident to Irenaeus was the historical character of the Christian faith. For Irenaeus, the faith was not so much a series of doctrines as it was a series of acts and promises of God.[7] Since such acts and promises cannot be changed, and the four gospels are the historical witness to the crucial events of the life of Jesus, they too cannot be changed. Although in much of this chapter I have underscored the divergences among the four gospels, it is obvious that they were brought together into a single canon primarily because of their convergences. And their central point of convergence is the historical Jesus. All of them, each in its own fashion, bear witness to Jesus and to the historical facts surrounding his life, teachings, and work. In general, though often for other reasons, most Christians have accepted this element of closure, so that no new gospels can be added to the canon.

On the other hand, there is in this view of the canon an element of openness we often miss.[8] The multiplicity of the gospels implies that their witness can never be contained in a single, fixed expression. Throughout the ages, the multiplicity of the gospels has produced a discomfort similar to what I felt in my high school years. If there were only one gospel, things would be simpler. Hans Lietzmann has expressed the difficulties and the early attempted solutions quite well:

> The fact of there being four gospels, however, had its disadvantages. As far as the Church was concerned, there was only *one* gospel, only one message of God to mankind, and the question arose as to why it was divided up among four books. Further, why were there so many repetitions, and also incompatibilities and apparent contradictions, in the various gospels? Surely the ideal state of affairs would be *one* gospel in *one* book. That was perhaps the case in the earliest period when the Synoptic gospels were confined, each to different regions, some using one gospel and some another. Marcion had permitted only one gospel book to be used in his church. About A.D. 180 two men commenced a practice which the Church employs today, whenever popular preachers attempt to revitalize religion by teaching "Bible history"; out of the four records, they make a single text. The first to do this was bishop Theophilus of Antioch; his work has disappeared without trace. On the other hand, the second enjoyed great success: he was Tatian, a pupil of Justin. His gospel harmony of "the Four," known as the *Diatessaron,* arranges sections of all four gospels as a continuous gospel story. . .
>
> Nevertheless the Church as a whole refused to accept any such abbreviation of the gospel texts. The struggle against the arbitrariness of Marcion and gnosticism had shown her the value of a tradition founded on a good historical basis. . . . The four gospels were thus kept intact.[9]

It is in this resistance to "abbreviation" that the value of the fourfold witness to the gospel lies. Precisely because there are four gospels, irreducible to a single one, every attempt at systematizing the gospel falls short of its goal, just as a true harmony of the four gospels is unattainable. There is always an element that is left aside, something needing correction.

If there were only one witness to the gospel, one could claim that a particular exposition of the Christian faith encompasses all of it. But since there are these irreducible witnesses, it follows that by definition the true "catholic" faith is pluralistic. It is "according to the whole," not in the sense that it encompasses the whole in a single, systematic, entirely coherent unit, but rather in the sense that it allows for the openness, for the testimony of plural perspectives and experiences, which is implied in the fourfold canonical witness to the gospel.

According to the passage from Irenaeus that we have studied, one of the marks of heresy is precisely that it refuses to accept this multiform witness to the gospel. It yields to the common temptation to have a gospel and a theology that can be managed and controlled—as Lietzmann would say, an "abbreviated" form of the gospel. Heresy, as opposed to true catholicity, to the gospel "according to the whole," consists precisely in raising a partial vision to the category of the absolute. It is for this reason that when the term "catholic" loses its dimension of openness, and becomes synonymous with a rigid orthodoxy believing itself to encompass all truth, it in fact becomes heretical. It is heretical because, like the ancient heretics who sought to make the gospel more manageable by reducing the gospels to a single one, it believes that it can produce a single, universal theology, encompassing the entire gospel and valid everywhere and at all times, as if the quadriform witness to the gospel were incidental and could be surpassed by an overarching synthesis.

THE FOURFOLD GOSPEL AND
THE MULTIPLE WITNESS OF SCRIPTURE

The multiplicity of the gospels implies that, although they do have great authority, they are not "fallen from heaven." All of them are equally valid witnesses to the gospel of Jesus Christ. Yet each of them reflects the particular circumstances and perspectives of the Christian community in which it was born. This has implications, not only for our understanding of the gospels, but also for our understanding of the nature of biblical revelation. Precisely because there are four gospels, the authority of the Bible is different from the authority of a Greek oracle or of the Koran. The multiplicity of the gospels, all included in the single canon of the New Testament, means that no one of them, by itself, contains the complete and final witness to the gospel of Jesus Christ. It also means that every witness to that gospel takes place from a particular perspective and reflects the concrete circumstances in which it takes place. Because there are four gospels, and they do not always agree among themselves, we are unable to claim that the New Testament was handed down from heaven in its final form, and that all we can do now is copy it over and over again.

This plural perspective of Scripture is exemplified by the fourfold witness to the gospel, but not limited to it. On the contrary, throughout Scripture one finds a multiplicity of perspectives on the same issues and events. Already in the very first chapters of Genesis, there are two different accounts of creation. In one, God creates animals first, and humankind last (Gen. 1:24-26). In another, the man is created first, then the animals, and finally the woman (Gen. 2:7-8, 18-22). Obviously, both cannot be true in the sense of being a literal account of the order of creation.[10] The same is the case throughout the Pentateuch, where several stories are repeated, though with different slants and details. Later, when the time comes to name a king, some texts tell us that this was the will of God (I Samuel 9), and others say the opposite (I Samuel 8). Indeed, throughout the historical books, there are several parallel accounts of a number of events, agreeing in the essential, but differing both in details and in the interpretation of the significance of the event.

When it came to telling the story of the beginning of creation, the ancient Israelites followed an interesting procedure. They collected stories and traditions that already circulated in the Near East, purged and adapted them so they would reflect Israel's understanding of God and of the world, and put them together into what eventually became sacred Scripture. Apparently, what was important to them was not the uniqueness of the story, but the uniqueness of God and the singleness of creation. For this reason, they ended up with more than one story about how the one God made the one creation. The tensions and contradictions among the stories apparently did not bother them, and they were quite ready to include the various stories within the one canon of sacred Scripture.

Many modern scholars now tell us that these various stories had a multitude of origins, some having been borrowed by the people of Israel from other neighboring peoples. Apparently, some of these stories were more popular in a particular tribe or region. When the present text of Scripture was composed, these different stories were sometimes combined, and sometimes simply placed side by side—as in the case of the two creation stories in Genesis 1 and 2.

Clearly, once these stories came to form part of the sacred canon, first Jews and then Christians agreed that there was something normative about them. Yet the very fact that there was more than one story should have led to the openness for which I argue here.

Instead of this, however, what Christian orthodoxy most often did was to ignore the differences among these various stories, compile them into a single one that was different from any of the stories found in the sacred text, and implicitly claim that this one compiled story was the only orthodox possibility.

Such an understanding of the nature of Scripture and of catholicity has led, not only to the Scopes trial and to "scientific creationism," but also to a number of interesting incidents, such as the one told by a Sioux physician:

> A missionary once undertook to instruct a group of Indians in the truths of his holy religion. He told them of the creation of the earth in six days, and of the fall of our first parents by eating an apple.
> The courteous savages listened attentively, and, after thanking him, one

related in his turn a very ancient tradition concerning the origin of maize. But the missionary plainly showed his disgust and disbelief, indignantly saying:

"What I delivered to you were sacred truths, but this that you tell me is mere fable and falsehood!"

"My brother," gravely replied the offended Indian, "it seems that you have not been well grounded in the rules of civility. You saw that we, who practice these rules, believed your stories; why, then, do you refuse to credit ours?"[11]

The point here, however, is not simply that the missionary appeared intolerant. The point is rather that the attitude of the supposed unbeliever toward the stories of origins was probably closer to that of the original composer or writer of Genesis than was the missionary's. In Genesis 1 and 2, two different stories of creation are placed side by side. They represent different tribal traditions. They also speak the truth of creation by the one God. Who was more biblical, the missionary who insisted that his *one* story of creation was the only true one, or the Indian who was ready to accept that story as well as others?

Therefore, what is true of the gospels is true of the Bible as a whole. Throughout Scripture one finds the diversity of perspectives and of interpretations that my friend Silvino pointed out in the gospels, and that I found so embarrassing.

From my earlier perspective as a young student trying to convert my classmates, this was a decided disadvantage. My task would have been much easier if I had been able to produce a single document, with no inner tensions or contradictions. For similar reasons, there have always been in the church those who ignore the tensions among the four gospels, and attempt to read the New Testament as if it were a Koran, fallen from heaven or dictated by God without regard for particular human circumstances, experiences, or perspectives.[12]

To do so, however, is to ignore the very nature of the Bible and of the faith to which it witnesses. The Bible is plural. Indeed, the very name, *ta Biblia,* from which we derive our English "Bible," is plural, meaning not "the Book," as we now say, but "the book*s*." The theology of each of the gospels is different from that of the others, and they are all different from Paul's, Jude's, or James'.

IMPLICATIONS FOR A PLURALISTIC THEOLOGY

Simply and boldly stated, what this means is that the opposite of a pluralistic church and a pluralistic theology is not simply an exclusivistic church and a rigid theology, but a heretical church and a heretical theology! We may resent the problems created by the existence in our canon of four gospels that do not agree; but those four gospels are there precisely to keep us from the easy assumption that we can somehow create, or that we have inherited, a theology that encompasses all truth. Uncomfortable as this is, it is a reminder of the absolute catholicity or universality of the gospel, which cannot be encompassed by any one perspective, any one theology, or any one culture. As missiologist Lamin Sanneh has stated, "For all of us pluralism can be a rock of stumbling, but for God it is the cornerstone of the universal design."[13]

Thus, the ultimate reason why a "Roundtable of Ethnic Theologians" is necessary, or why it is important for the church at large to listen to the plural perspectives we and others bring to the table, is that, just as the gospel is attested in Scripture by a multiform witness, so must it be interpreted and lived today through the multiform witness of many perspectives, so that it may be truly "catholic"—according to the whole. Although the Gospel of Mark is God's word to us today, we would lose much if we had only it, and not the other three. The same is true for Matthew, Luke, and John. Likewise, though the church is truly the church wherever it is, it too loses much when it is limited to a single perspective, which then appears to be final, complete, and universally applicable.

This must serve as a caution, not only to traditional theology, but also to the various theologies that are emerging out of different perspectives, and to those who seek to incorporate the insights of such perspectives into the theological mainstream. Each of these theologies has significant contributions to make to the whole, and it is to be hoped that, as it is brought before the roundtable of varying perspectives, each of our theologies will be enriched. This does not mean, however, that what we must now do is simply to bring together all the contributions of these various perspectives, in order then to forge a truly "universal" theology. Such a "universal" theology, were it achievable, would lack true catholicity, for the same reason that a "harmony" of the gospels, one in which all differences are resolved, must never be substituted for the fourfold witness to the gospel. When used in this manner, "universal," rather than a synonym for "catholic," is its antonym. Along these lines, the words of Jung Young Lee at the 1987 session of the Roundtable bear quoting: "It is not, therefore, possible to construct a theology for everyone. . . . I am not suggesting a theological paradigm for the whole church. If I do, I am as guilty as the traditional dogmatic theologians who attempt to provide valid theological thinking for the whole church."[14]

Furthermore, given the manner in which a particular group's perspective necessarily influences its theology, there is always the likelihood that any theology that claims to be "universal" is no more than theology from the particular perspective of those who are in power. This is the reason for what Cain H. Felder calls "the total inadequacy and racial tendentiousness of the West's intellectual tradition in its endeavors to provide allegedly *universal* conceptual and religious norms." [15]

It is for this reason that in the chapters that follow, while seeking to express some of the variety that has emerged in the Ethnic Theologians' Roundtable, and to show the importance of some of the insights shared in it, I have refrained from attempting to bring all such insights into a systematic whole. Our purpose as ethnic theologians has been to produce, not a better and more "universal" theology, but one—or rather, several— that are more truly catholic.

MISSION AND THE CATHOLIC VOCATION OF CHRISTIAN THEOLOGY

In our missionary speeches, we often ground the missionary enterprise on the "Great Commission," as it appears at the end of the Gospel of Matthew. However, the very possibility of that commission, and its nature, are closely related to the multiplicity of the gospels that witness to the gospel, and the multiplicity of perspectives in the entire Bible. The fact that there are four "gospels," and that from them we may derive different conclusions and perspectives, is of fundamental importance for the Christian missionary enterprise.

Precisely because the gospels are four, and the theologies of the New Testament are many, the gospel can be translated—both in a literal and in a figurative sense.

In a literal sense, it is significant that traditionally the Christian church has not objected to the translation of Scripture into other languages. Quite the contrary, throughout the ages, and even to this day, missionaries have reduced countless languages to writing, and their primary purpose in so doing has been to translate the Bible into those languages. The resulting translations also are considered to be "the Bible," and they do not lack authority because they are in a language different from that of the original Scriptures. True, one may debate about the best possible translation of a word or phrase, and in this sense some translations are ·better than others. Yet a translation does not have to wait until it is certified as "exact"—which would in any case be impossible—before it can claim biblical authority. Every translation is an interpretation; and yet, a translation is still "the Bible."

The Koran may be put into another language; but the result is not the Koran itself. The true book from heaven is the Arabic original. Correspondingly, the expansion of Islam, especially in the first centuries after its inception, has usually been connected with the expansion of the Arabic language. In contrast, according to a tradition of long standing in the Christian church, a translated Bible is still the Bible. Throughout history, Christian missionaries have sought to make the message of Scripture available by translating the Bible, rather than by requiring that their new and prospective converts learn the biblical languages.[16]

In a figurative sense, the "translatability" of the gospels implies also the "translatability" of the gospel. Missiologist Lamin Sanneh has expressed the contrasts between these two approaches:

> There are two basic ways to proceed. One is to make the missionary culture the inseparable carrier of the message. This we might call mission by *diffusion*. By it religion expands from its original cultural base and is implanted in other societies primarily as a matter of cultural identity. Islam, with which Christianity shares a strong missionary tradition, exemplifies this mode of mission. It carries with it certain inalienable cultural assumptions, such as the indispensability of its Arabic heritage in Scripture, law and religion.
>
> The other way is to make the recipient culture the true and final locus of the proclamation, so that the religion arrives without the presumption of cultural rejection. This we might call mission by *translation*. It carries with it a deep theological vocation, which arises as an inevitable stage in the process of reception and adaptation.[17]

These contrasting approaches to mission stem from different views on the nature of sacred scripture: the Koran is a single book; the Bible is a series of books and includes a variety of perspectives and interpretations of the events with which it deals.

Christianity is based on the fourfold witness to the gospel, and on a Bible that includes a similar diversity of perspectives. For such a religion, "catholicity" is crucial, and this catholicity means, not only being present throughout the world, but also being a faith "according to the whole"—meaning, in the New Testament, according to the whole witness of all four evangelists, and, in the best times of its history, according to the perspective, experience, and witness of all the *oikoumene*.

In brief, the Christian missionary enterprise is based on two poles, both equally important, but one often forgotten. On the one hand—and this has been emphasized most often—the Christian missionary enterprise is based on the need of "the nations." As Christians, we are convinced that . the gospel is indeed Good News that all should hear, and which we must proclaim to all. On the other hand, the Christian missionary enterprise is also based on the catholic vocation of the gospel. To paraphrase Irenaeus, just as there are four gospels which in their multiplicity witness to the one gospel, it is necessary that believers from all the four corners of the earth bring the richness of their experience and perception of the gospel, so that we may all come to a fuller, more "catholic"—"according to the whole"—understanding of the gospel. The church calls all the "nations" to the gospel, not only because the "nations" need the gospel, but also because the church needs the "nations" in order to be fully "catholic." If "catholic" means "according to the whole," as long as a part of the whole remains outside, or is brought in without being allowed to speak from its own perspective, catholicity itself is truncated.

CHRISTIANITY AND CULTURE

As a result of this understanding of its sacred scripture and of the revelation available through it, the Christian missionary enterprise has usually been surprisingly open to inculturation.[18] Quite clearly, the degree and the manner in which such inculturation ought to take place has never been an easy matter to resolve. In India, for instance, the early Portuguese Catholic missionaries have been faulted for seeking to turn their converts into Portuguese—giving them Portuguese names, attire, and so forth. On the other hand, in the same country, the later Italian Jesuits also have been criticized for carrying inculturation to the point of declaring that the caste system was a purely cultural matter, having little to do with the gospel, so that the church could accept it, having separate services and congregations for different castes. Similar debates have ensued wherever the Christian message has encountered a new culture. In Japan, the issue was whether Shintoism was a political-cultural or a religious matter. In China, the so-called ancestor worship was one of many issues so debated. In Africa, polygamy posed similar questions. Various groups and denominations take different stances on these issues. However, the point here is not the particular stance they take. The point is rather that in every case the issue of inculturation, and how it should proceed, is crucial for Christian mission, and this to a degree that is not true of other world religions.

Today it has become quite commonplace to point out the degree to which missionaries and their converts confused the culture of the missionaries with the gospel. We all know a number of horror stories: Spanish missionaries in the sixteenth century receiving instructions from Queen Isabella to discourage among their converts the unholy practice of taking daily baths. Attempts by nineteenth-century missionaries to "clothe the savages," even though their traditional attire was better suited to the local climate than the European garb imposed upon them. Protestants in Latin America who would drink tea rather than coffee, because that was the preferred beverage of the missionaries who first came to them.

On the other hand, the very fact that we now recognize all these as horror stories is indicative of the contradiction between such procedures and the very nature of Christianity. When one stops to reflect about it, it is indeed odd how followers of an avowedly and unashamedly missionary religion such as Christianity can be so critical of missionary efforts that have gained so many converts. The reason for this is that there is something in Christianity that makes the forced acculturation of its converts repugnant to itself—even though historically it has often and repeatedly practiced such forced acculturation.[19] When Christians, particularly those whose Christian confession is the result of colonial and cultural imperialism, criticize and bewail that manner in which those who brought the gospel to them also brought a foreign culture, they do so, not only out of a sense of cultural or national identity, but also out of their understanding of the gospel itself.

H. Richard Niebuhr's *Christ and Culture* has made a significant contribution to Christian reflection on the relationship between faith and one's culture. To this day, several decades after it was written, it is a useful introduction to such issues. There is, however, a crucial point which must be made, and which is often neglected in such discussions: The knowledge of Christ never comes to us apart from culture, or devoid of cultural baggage. Christ comes to us in the garb of Christianity; and Christianity, in all its various forms, already involves an inculturation of the faith. To speak of "Christ and culture," as if Christ ever came to anyone apart from culture, is to oversimplify the matter. A Christ without culture is a docetic, non-incarnate Christ. Thus, Niebuhr's "Christ against culture" is not really such, but is rather the Christ of a particular culture (usually an ecclesiastical, and even sectarian culture) against the dominant culture. When Tertullian, for instance, spoke of the distance between Christianity and Roman culture, he was speaking of the distance between the culture of the church in North Africa and the dominant culture of the Roman Empire.

From its very inception, the gospel was proclaimed within a culture. Jesus came to his contemporaries within the circumstances of the Jewish culture of his time and place. It was as Jews—more concretely, as Galilean Jews—that his first disciples received him. Ever since, in the passage to the various forms of Hellenistic culture, in the conversion of the Germanic peoples, and in every other missionary enterprise and conversion experience, people have met Christ mediated through cultures—both theirs and the culture of those who communicated the gospel to them.

> There is no such thing as a chemically pure "gospel," not translated into a culture. . . . The encounter between Gospel and culture can only take place through the Church, that is to say, through a historical construct that is already socio-culturally conditioned. In truth, there is no encounter between

Gospel and culture, but rather between Church and culture, that is, between carriers of different socio-cultural traditions.[20]

This is a very important point to remember as we approach the subject of this entire book. There is always the danger, on the part of a dominant culture, not to see the degree to which its understanding of the faith is itself culturally conditioned. In the most blatant cases, the result is the long series of "horror stories" in mission to which I have already referred. But there is a more subtle manner in which cultural imperialism functions, usually without the knowledge of those who practice it—or even of those who suffer it.

This more subtle cultural imperialism usually presents itself as a missiological theory in which the notion of "translation" is dominant. What has already been said regarding the "translatability" of the gospel has often led to the notion, on the part of Christians of a dominant culture, or of a culture sending missionaries into another, that in order to "translate" the gospel into another culture what they must do is to separate the gospel from the cultural garb in which it exists in the dominant or sending culture, and then reclothe it in another culture. The truth, however, is not that simple. For persons to assume that they can disengage that which is essential in their Christianity from that which is culturally conditioned is to assume too much. No one is that free from cultural bias—much less those who, because of their privileged position, seldom see their cultural presuppositions questioned.

Obviously, given the need to communicate the gospel in different settings, attempts at translation are not only justifiable, but also necessary. Yet, it is important to point out that, if the translators take themselves too seriously, believing that they have somehow discerned the core of the gospel and translated it into another culture, they will be guilty of the same oversimplification of the gospel that was characteristic of those early heretics for whom the quadriform witness to the gospel was a stumbling block. Just as the gospel cannot be separated from this plural and even confusing witness and reduced to a single, monophonic witness, so can it not be separated from the various cultures in which it takes flesh.[21]

This, however, is not the greatest danger for those whose theology reflects the dominant culture. The greatest danger is to forget that the same questions that must be asked regarding the inculturation of Christianity in non-Western cultures must also be asked regarding its dominant inculturation in the West. The question of Christianity and culture is not only a missiological question, to be posed in those instances where Christianity crosses cultural boundaries. It is also a crucial theological question for Christianity in those areas and cultures in which it is dominant. Yet, it is a question seldom asked.

It is important to clarify the nature of this question. The question is not, How should Christianity relate to culture in the United States in the last decade of the twentieth century? That is certainly an important question. The culture around us is changing, and the church must give careful consideration to its response to such changes. The question of the manner in which Christianity ought to relate to culture is essentially the same as Niebuhr's question in *Christ and Culture*. But this is not the question to which I am referring. Indeed, the very posing of the question in such terms is an indication that we have not understood the fundamental issue. It takes for granted that one somehow knows what Christianity is apart from culture, and that what one must then inquire about is how such Christianity should be brought to bear on a changing culture. The "Christ" of the Christ and culture question is of necessity the Christ of a culture. Therefore, to ask how Christianity ought to relate to culture begs the earlier questions: To what extent is our present understanding of Christianity determined by our culture? How does our culture limit our understanding of Christianity? How should such an understanding be corrected?

When ethnic minority or Third World theologians look at the dominant theologies of the West, they see a degree of inculturation of which Western theologians themselves are often not aware. Stephen S. Kim pointed this out at one of the meetings of the Roundtable, while insisting also on the need for reconciliation:

> It must be made known that the Western churches and their theologies fell prey to the influence of capitalistic, imperialistic ideologies, and participated in, or at least acquiesced to, the expansionist oppression policies of the West. Western theologies are called theologies of the oppressors because as the West conquered the world in the past few centuries in terms of military, economic, and cultural power, its churches and theologies failed to proclaim the prophetic judgments against the evils of capitalism and imperialism. One caveat is that today's oppressor can easily be tomorrow's oppressed. We want to do theology for the oppressed not to scorn or fight the West but to dialogue in search of the more holistic, more just, more humane, authentic community in which we all are but destined to coexist.[22]

Theologians representing the dominant culture seldom ask questions about their theology that would lead them to see what Dr. Kim is saying here. They should be forced to do so both by the obvious alienness of Scripture and by the existence of a *catholic* church, which does not always share the perceptions of the dominant culture. Yet it is easy to avoid such questions. For obvious reasons—including the economic realities of the publishing enterprise—the dialogue among theologians of the dominant culture seems to overshadow any theological work or perceptions by others. One way in which the challenge of other cultures and perspectives is avoided is by devoting one's attention to increasingly specialized or abstract topics, as is currently happening in some of our supposedly "best" schools of theology—a modern version of the ancient question about angels dancing on the head of a pin. When others interpret the Christian faith in terms of their own culture and traditions, those in the dominant culture often see such interpretations as quaint or even interesting; but they seldom ask themselves how such interpretations of the Christian faith should influence or change their own. Without asking that question, no theology can be truly *catholic*. And without a catholic, universal approach to its own theology, the church itself rapidly becomes parochial, even though it may be present throughout the world. As African theologian John S. Mbiti has expressed it,

> As the Church becomes worldwide, as it affirms the universality for which God's dispersal of history has destined it, let those of us who are its sons and daughters, and who are privileged to be its theologians, also think big, think far in time and space. Theology should strain its neck to see beyond the horizons of our traditional structures, beyond the comforts of our ready-made methodologies of theologizing; it should be with the Church where it is, rubbing shoulders with human beings whose condition, outlook, concerns, and world views are not those with which we are familiar.[23]

One of the goals of the Roundtable of Ethnic Theologians has been precisely to pose such a challenge, not only to itself, but also to the church at large, and in particular to those among its theologians who represent the dominant culture and whose thinking tends to be limited by those cultural parameters. After all, if theology in the United States is to be, as Mbiti says, where the church is, it will find it increasingly necessary to be where the church is actually growing, namely, in our ghettos, our barrios, and all our minority communities.

On the other hand, there is also the danger, on the part of those representing non-dominant cultures—or cultures which, though dominant in their countries of origin, are not traditionally Christian—that, in our attempts to rediscover and reaffirm elements of our traditional culture long since suppressed, we may fall into the trap of romanticizing culture.

Such romanticization of culture commonly takes two forms. One is to idealize one's culture, as if it were perfect and did not stand in need of correction from the gospel. This is an understandable reaction on the part of those who have repeatedly been told that their culture was incompatible with Christianity, and now find otherwise. When various peoples become Christian, they do not—they cannot—leave their culture behind, no matter how much they are told that they ought to do so, and no matter how hard they strive to meet such a goal. Culture is not something one can put on and take off, like a winter coat. "Culture is not a mere refinement that is added unto one's being, nor a valuable, though inaccessible, inheritance of traditions. It is rather an entire pattern or design for life in which the identity of each of its members is at stake." [24] For this reason, one should not be surprised if sincere Christians who have sought to leave behind their ancestral cultures, when finally convinced that such efforts were not necessary, react by romanticizing that culture, claiming for it a perfection it never had, and one they themselves would not claim had it not been for their own frustration with the dominant, supposedly "Christian" culture.

Every culture, though a God-given gift, has also been tainted by sin. Furthermore, in the origin itself of our various cultures there is a history of oppressions we must not idealize. The fact that I speak Spanish is the result of a long series of conquests, some dating back more than a thousand years. In these conquests, people were subjugated and even obliterated. I speak Spanish because Castile conquered Andalusia. I speak Spanish because some of my Spanish ancestors conquered and oppressed some of my Native American ancestors. I speak Spanish because, for whatever reasons, my native ancestors were among those who capitulated before the military, cultural, and religious onslaught of Spain. Therefore, even though I love my language and the sentiments it can express, I must not idealize my own culture to such a degree that I forget the many oppressions and injustices through which it was forged. I expect that, if we go back far enough, we shall find similar origins to other cultures. Africans were sold into slavery by other Africans, and some Native American cultures built empires at the expense of neighboring peoples. Also, for a number of reasons, many traditional cultures have proved quite oppressive of women. On this score, the warning of Robert Schreiter is in order:

> Cultural romanticism will tend to see only good in a culture and to believe that the ideal state of the culture would be reached if it were left untouched by the outside world. To be sure, the more intimately acquainted one becomes with a culture and the more one sees its delicate balancing of forces, the more one can become entranced by its beauty. But to fall prey to this kind of romanticism assumes that there is no sin in the world, that people cannot be and are not often cruel to one another, and that culture contact is always a bad thing. One should remember that, if Christianity is alive at all in a situation, it will certainly change things about the culture. The Christian message, after all, is about change: repentance, salvation, and an eschatological reality to be realized. To think that Christianity will not change a situation is to rob the Christian message of its most important part.[25]

The other danger on the part of those seeking to rediscover the value and significance of their culture is to fall into a static understanding of culture. Culture, when it is relevant, is a living thing. Like all living things,

it affects its environment and is affected by it. Although cultures are by
nature slow to change, for they encompass the wisdom of centuries, only a
dead culture ceases to change. Thus, when "indigenization shades into
antiquarianism," [26] one suspects that the culture being defended and
restored is no longer a living one, but rather a museum piece. Cultures
interact. Such interaction does not always have positive results, and more
often than not it reflects impositions brought about by military or economic force. Yet the result of such interaction is that old cultures take new
shapes, and new cultures are also born.

In summary, Harvey Cox is right when he declares that

> the trouble with most currently popular theological inculturation theories is
> that they overlook two important things. One is that cultures can be stifling
> and oppressive to many of the people who have to live in them. The other is
> that cultures everywhere are changing at an accelerated speed.[27]

It seems to me, however, that Cox misreads the interaction of cultures
in the world today when he seems to imply that a single world culture is
emerging. True, the impact of technology, and the overwhelming power
of a global economy, can be seen almost everywhere. True, all cultures are
being affected by these factors, and to that extent a commonality is
spreading. But as is characteristic of middle-class white Westerners, Cox
underestimates the power of ancestral cultural traditions when he
declares:

> Haltingly, and in spurts, a new global symbol system is coming into view. It is
> largely the creation of people under 25, the majority of the world's popula-
> tion. It is often subversive of existing dominant cultures. There will be losses,
> but it is fully capable of carrying into the future what is humanly valuable
> about the past, and not in the cultural equivalent of wildlife sanctuaries. It
> would be too bad if just as Christianity is becoming—for the first time—a
> truly world religion, we encased ourselves in the confines of a passing age
> instead of embracing the dangerous dawning of a new one.[28]

There is a mysteriously atavistic element in culture. Why is it that the
ancient symbols, dances, and rites of my Native American ancestors, which
I never learned at school nor in the family, still cause a stirring in me?
Why is it that worship becomes more meaningful when those symbols are
present? Somehow, in a manner that I cannot explain, I am an heir to a
culture my Spanish ancestors thought they had obliterated, and which my
European-oriented teachers did not believe was worth preserving or teaching. Quite clearly, there is also much in my culture that comes from Spain.
But that imported culture has not eliminated a strange, mysteriously beau-
tiful residue that I cannot explain in terms other than cultural atavism.

That is where the power of culture lies. Cultures change, adapt to one another, sometimes are even suppressed; but they do not die easily. We may be in an age of world communications, but people hear what is being communicated through their cultural ears. The young people in a "hot spot" in Alajuela whose attire and musical preferences prompted Harvey Cox's remarks are still very Costa Rican. They may imitate North American rock singers and dress like the teenagers they see on television, but they are still part of an ancient culture forged through centuries of struggle with the world and with others. That will not simply disappear because young people all over the world listen to rock music and wear jeans. Such things will certainly influence and shape ancient cultures, but they will not make them disappear. They may create new worldwide symbols; but those symbols will not erase the ancient ones, nor will they be free from significant shifts in meaning according to the culture into which they are grafted.

We must neither romanticize ancient cultures nor allow ourselves to be overwhelmed by the challenges the present-day world communications market poses to them. Cultures are such precisely because they have survived many a challenge. A strong, living culture will most likely survive the challenges of modernity (or postmodernity) as well as any challenge we might pose to it by pointing to its imperfections.

The theologians who have gathered at the Roundtable have not done so as apologists for our various cultures. We know that cultures are not normally transferable. I cannot simply persuade others to come join my culture. Nor can I divest myself of my culture and join theirs. At best, I can interpret my culture to others so that they may see that it is worthy of respect, and that it may have something to contribute to human well-being. And they can interpret their culture to me, so that I may glimpse some of its worth and beauty, and come to respect its actual and potential contribution to humankind. As representatives of cultures that have often been colonized and oppressed, we find it necessary to insist on this point, for throughout history—and to this day—others have sought to impose their culture on us. This has often been done under the guise of evangelization. Our ancestors were told that there was a "Christian" culture, and that in order to accept it they had to reject their own. Even today, in myriad ways, we are being told the same. Such notions we unreservedly reject.

We have come rather as Christian theologians who confess and rejoice that our cultural identities and experiences have given us particular perspectives and insights into the meaning of the gospel. We seek to call the entire church to an understanding of itself and of its message that is more truly catholic.

It is important, however, to understand the vision of catholicity implied in this last statement. We do not call for the development of a new, more inclusive universal theology, into which our various insights would be incorporated so as to form a new orthodoxy to be accepted by all. We call rather for a theological stance similar to that of the early church when it made provision for the fourfold witness to the gospel. Just as the conversation among the four gospels can never be reduced to a "harmony" of the gospels, so should the dialogue at the ethnic roundtable never be reduced to a new "universal" theology. Just as the four gospels stand in the way of any proposed "abbreviation" of the gospel, so let our continuing dialogue, our various perspectives, our agreements and disagreements, stand in the way of any proposed "universal" theology—which would soon become an instrument for the oppression of those who disagree.

On this score, an excellent example is the attitude expressed by Jung Young Lee in a paper he presented at the very first session of the Roundtable. After arguing convincingly for the value of yin-yang as a theological paradigm (to which we shall return later), he adds:

> I want to make clear that I am not arguing for a theological paradigm for the whole church. If I do, I am as guilty as the traditional dogmatic theologians who attempt to provide valid theological thinking for the whole church. . . . Even if the yin-yang symbol has a universal implication, it is not my intention to insist on it as a universal paradigm for the whole church. Perhaps, an important service I can render to the church in presenting this theological paradigm is to assist other theologians in finding their own paradigms which can also help them realize the particularity and the universality of the Christian faith.[29]

Ours is a vision of catholicity; of catholicity so far-reaching that it can never be reduced to uniform universality. It is from this *singular* vision of catholicity that we offer the *plural* visions that follow.

CHAPTER THREE

VISIONS OF THE WORD

When Silvino accosted me in my high school years, taunting me about the different versions of events in the gospels, he showed that I did not have a very clear idea how to interpret Scripture. He also showed that, if I was to be honest and effective in my interpretation of Scripture, I needed to devise a new hermeneutics.

In a way, the same is true of all of us as we come to the realization that, as ethnic minorities, we have something unique to contribute to the church and its theology. To ground that contribution in Scripture, and relate it to the entire tradition of Christian theology, we must devise an appropriate hermeneutics. For that reason, the first topic the Roundtable addressed was biblical hermeneutics. The invitation sent to prospective presenters of papers defined the purpose of the discussion as follows:

> It is hoped that presenters will deal with questions such as: How does our ethnic experience and/or cultural background illumine Scripture? Do we (or should we) read Scripture differently? How? What are some approaches and/or methodologies that help us in such interpretation? Are there texts that acquire a particular meaning or significance from our perspective?

POINTS OF AGREEMENT

The four papers that were presented, each from the perspective of one of the principal ethnic minority groups, as well as the discussion that followed, showed remarkable agreement among all participants, particularly on four central points:

1) The Bible has traditionally been interpreted in ways that are oppressive to minorities and to powerless groups, and that serve to justify the actions and values of the oppressors.

2) There is need for a new hermeneutics, and this must be based on an entirely different approach to biblical scholarship and interpretation.

3) There are elements in our traditional cultures that bring us closer than much Western theology to the biblical world view.

4) A crucial aspect of this new hermeneutics will be a communal approach.

I shall highlight some of the main elements under each of these headings, and then move to more general issues regarding hermeneutics from minority perspectives, and its connection with what was said in the foregoing chapter regarding catholicity and the quadriform witness to the gospel.

THE BIBLE AS A TOOL OF OPPRESSION

It was Homer Noley, a Choctaw, who most strongly emphasized this point. In his paper, "Native Americans and the Hermeneutical Task," he underscored the role of "theological presuppositions and constructions which were put in place by Colonial America to describe the place of Native Americans in the nation's theological themes."[1] He pointed out, among other things, that in *The History of the Work of Redemption,* Jonathan Edwards, dean of American theologians, affirmed that the inhabitants of the "promised land" were "wholly possessed of Satan until the coming of the Europeans."

That many of the early "settlers" held such views should be no news for any who know the early religious history of this nation. Noley adds, however, that these opinions did not die out with the eighteenth century, nor have they been reserved to obscure cultural corners populated by obvious bigots. As late as the mid–twentieth century, Peter Marshall, Jr., and David Manuel published a book entitled *The Light and the Glory.*[2] They set out to answer the question, "Did God have a plan for America?" In this book, the authors claim that God's plan was that this country would be a "new Jerusalem," and that this was "to be worked out in terms of the settlers' covenant with God and with each other." In that scheme, when Marshall and Manuel refer to the "Indians," these are usually listed together with droughts and with smallpox, as "enemies from which God delivered his people." When the pronoun "we" is employed, it certainly does not include the native inhabitants of the land. Furthermore, those inhabitants are not even considered human, as when the authors declare that God "had withheld it [the New World] from man's knowledge this long, in almost virginal purity." All of this, Marshall and Manuel justify with abundant biblical quotations, particularly those referring to the Promised Land, the extermination of the Canaanites, and so on.

Along the same lines, Korean American Stephen S. Kim declared that theology has in the past been found always trailing the world and history, not leading them as was once the case with the Old Testament prophets. It was used and abused to justify someone's social, political, cultural programmes. . . . Trapped, so to speak, by the ideological and political agendas of the ruling party, the Church and its conscience have in large measure, excepting of course a few conscientious objectors, remained domesticated and without challenging prophecy. Thus became the Church the solicitor and supplicator for the states when they turned colonial and imperialistic in seventeenth and eighteenth century Europe. Thus the Church said its blessings and invocations for the benefit of the powers which in return tolerated it. Thus their theology became the theology of the oppressors, the theology of the imperialist ideology.[3]

In my own paper, "Hermeneutics: A Hispanic Perspective," I pointed out that the manner in which the Bible is read and taught in most American churches shows a "selective forgetfulness" which parallels a similar forgetfulness in the reading of American history.[4] This selective forgetfulness is the handmaiden of injustice, which "thrives on the myth that the present order is somehow the result of pure intentions and a guiltless history." Examples of this "selective forgetfulness" are the manner in which David and Solomon are depicted only as great kings, while their sins are ignored, and the ease with which we read the genealogy of Jesus in Matthew, without recognizing the "skeletons in the closet" of that genealogy.

It was Cain H. Felder, however, who most systematically applied the methods of historical scholarship to show how even the most seemingly objective Western scholarship has been tainted by racism.[5] He declared that in 1980 he "began to realize that essentially my own theological training and graduate studies had treated most of ancient Africa as peripheral or insignificant." On the basis of this realization, he set out on a quest for those black African elements which traditional scholarship has ignored, but whose importance can be proved or at least defended on the basis of the same "scientific" tools.[6]

The results of this research are tantalizing, both for the new vistas they open, and for the clear implication that biblical scholarship, supposedly objective, has allowed itself to be guided, perhaps even subconsciously, by its racist presuppositions. He points out, for instance, that archaeological discoveries in what used to be called Nubia indicate that there was a "pharaonic" civilization and political organization in Nubia several generations before the First Dynasty of Egypt. It appears likely that Menes, the somewhat legendary founder of the First Egyptian Dynasty, was black. There are also records indicating that many of the pharaohs looked to Punt (Greater Ethiopia) as the land of origin of Egyptian civilization and of many Egyptian gods. Furthermore, not only was the Twenty-fifth Egyptian Dynasty, usually called "Nubian," black, but so were many of the pharaohs of the Eleventh and the Eighteenth to the Twenty-fifth dynasties—including Ramses II, "traditionally associated with Moses and the Exodus."

Felder is well aware that "the probability of the Pharaoh's 'blackness' turns out to be a two-edged sword."[7] It certainly shows that blacks can be as oppressive as any other people—and, as Felder suggests, may even serve as "a paradigm for reassessing the oppressive Black Pharaohs of the Black Church today."[8] His point, however, is that traditional Western scholarship has refused even to consider the possibility that Egyptian civilization may have come out of Africa. By creating the category of the "Middle East," which had very little historical reality before the Arab invasions, the black African connection is lost or at least obscured. A case in point is Bruce Metzger's affirmation (which Felder finds unsubstantiated) that "Semitic intruders from Southwest Arabia (Yemen) brought with them a more highly developed social organization, architecture and art as well as a system of writing."[9] Quoting Robert A. Bennett,[10] Felder declares that the claim that the ancient Egyptians and their civilization originated from peoples outside Africa is the result of "insidious racism."[11]

This is not to say that the Bible is itself oppressive, or even that it has always been interpreted in an oppressive fashion. On the contrary, in many a culture the biblical message, even when its liberating power has been limited by Western interpretations, has been liberating. Such was the case in Latin America when Protestantism first arrived and employed its preaching of the Bible to promote a more open society and a more participatory ecclesiology. Unfortunately, as time has passed and issues have changed, much of the message that was liberating at an earlier age has often become alienating and oppressive. Likewise, when the first Protestant missionaries arrived at a number of Asian cultures, what they had to say regarding the Bible and women was quite liberating. Unfortunately again, many a church has allowed itself to lose this liberating dimension of the message, usually by tying its own position regarding women to what was practiced in Western churches several decades ago, and reinforcing this with those elements of Confucianism which are oppressive of women.

THE CALL FOR A NEW HERMENEUTICS

From all the foregoing, it is clear that there is widespread agreement among ethnic minority theologians that there is need for a new hermeneutics. This must begin with a suspicion regarding received interpretations. As Felder put it, "The implication is that, whatever one may wish to say about the Bible, there is a need for a disciplined *skepticism* regarding its Western appropriations."[12] Homer Noley agrees: "If the Native American clergy are satisfied with their training, there may not be an interest in a new Biblical base for Native American ministries. If they are not satisfied, there is a place for Native American Biblical scholarship."[13] In my own paper, I recalled the general suspicion aroused in me when I discovered that a text I had heard interpreted since childhood had a very different meaning.[14]

This suspicion must be far-reaching and all-encompassing. Cain Felder suggests that it must be extended to include even the canon itself, which was compiled and determined by people with particular agendas, and with the power to push such agendas.[15] Traditional introductions to biblical studies often include a history of the canon; but they make little or no attempt to elucidate the political agendas involved in the decision to include or exclude a particular book.[16]

In this respect, the inclusion of the Deutero-Pauline material in the canon is instructive, as has been shown by Dennis R. MacDonald.[17] According to MacDonald, the Paul of the genuine epistles is much more open to the contribution and leadership of women, much more radical in his opposition to slavery, and much more democratic in his conception of the church, than the Paul of the Pastorals. Actually, there were a number of legends circulating about Paul, several of them in books that were eventually excluded from the canon, and which appear to be closer to the Paul of the epistles. Why were the Pastorals included in the canon, and the *Acts of Paul* and *Acts of Paul and Thecla* eventually excluded, even though they were considered canonical by some as late as the seventh century? Quite clearly, at least part of the reason is that the Paul of the Pastorals was safer for those in power than the Paul of the legends. Therefore, when we read the Paul of the genuine epistles through the lens of the Pastorals and other Deutero-Pauline material in the canon, we are reading him as those in power intended us to do. If, for instance, we read the Epistle to Philemon as an endorsement of slavery, it is because we are looking at it through the lens of the Deutero-Pauline material, and not of Galatians 3:28—and this is precisely as we were intended to read it by those who made the decisions about the canon.

It follows that this new hermeneutics must include a wider understanding of the Word of God. Noley's doubts about the possibility of devising a genuine Native American scholarship are grounded on the fact that most Native American clergy "reflect the fundamentalism of rural white non-Indian Christianity."[18] Felder expresses it as follows:

> While it is important for Black people to adopt rigorously a more critical stance toward traditional or prevailing exegetical methods and hermeneutical conclusions, more is required. Many persons must seek to liberate them-

selves from the popular tendency of *deifying* the Bible as *the* definitive and exclusive Word of God, as if God's entire revelation exists only in the canon of biblical literature. To be sure, the Bible does represent a foundation for the Word of God; moreover, from the faith claims of the Judaeo-Christian tradition the Bible does constitute the most important *ancient locus* for the Word of God. However, even this is not synonymous with the perspective that the Bible is *the* Word of God categorically.[19]

The notion that the Bible is *the* Word of God is not biblical. Nowhere does the Bible call itself the Word of God. The Bible does say, however, that there is an eternal Word of God: "In the beginning was the Word, and the Word was with God, and the Word was God." It then goes on to say that this Word is "the true light, which enlightens everyone," and that "the Word became flesh and lived among us" (John 1:1, 9, 14). This eternal Word of God, who enlightens everyone, was the basis on which ancient theology devised the doctrine of the Logos—the Greek term that our English Bibles translate as Word. Since this Logos enlightens everyone, it follows, so the ancients said, that wherever people have any light, they have it because of this eternal Word of God, who became incarnate in Jesus Christ. In its classical application, this doctrine was then used by the ancient church to claim for itself the wisdom of the Greek philosophers, for they too had been illumined by the same light or Word of God.

Had the church been consistent, this doctrine of the Logos should have been employed to affirm the cosmic connections of the Christ event. If the Word incarnate in Christ is the true light which enlightens everyone, it follows that the Word of God can be found wherever humans have any light whatsoever. But the church was not consistent. Once it attained a position of power within the Roman Empire and Greco-Roman culture—partially through its use of the doctrine of the Logos—it did not even consider the possibility that the same Word may have illumined those whom the "best" of culture considered "barbarians." *They* had no Logos. The Word had to be taken to them. Ever since, Christians seem to have remembered the doctrine of the Logos only when approaching cultures and civilizations they had no possibility of overpowering.[20] When, on the contrary, they faced cultures or civilizations they were determined to overrun, or which had not advanced the art of killing as Western civilization had, they saw in those cultures and civilizations nothing but idolatry and ignorance.

The ancient Christian doctrine of the Word or Logos of God, if applied without such considerations for power and convenience, would support Dr. Felder's claim that the Word of God is not limited to the canon of biblical literature. To be sure, that canon has a special place and authority in the Judeo-Christian tradition, and must be used as a means to judge whatever else one considers to be a manifestation of the Word of God. But the Word of God is older and infinitely more extensive than the canon of the Bible.

When Jonathan Edwards declared that the "savages" who inhabited these lands before the European invasion were possessed by Satan, and wholly devoid of any knowledge of God, he was denying the doctrine of the eternal and cosmic Word of God, which he accepted in other situations. Such contradiction, typical of traditional Christian approaches to Native Americans, black Africans, and most other peoples, betrays a hidden, non-theological agenda: the justification of the oppression and exploitation of supposedly inferior peoples and cultures.

Suppose, on the other hand, that we were to apply the traditional doctrine of the Logos, not only to the Greek philosophers, but also to the Native Americans, to black Africans before their encounter with Western civilization, and to the rest of humankind. In that case, the European invaders who came to these lands would have been forced to acknowledge the good that God had wrought here even before their arrival. Furthermore, if it is true that the Word of God is the source of any light, it follows that we must look for the activity and presence of the Word, not only in religious doctrines and practices, but also in the way in which people organize their lives and communities, love one another, care for the earth, and so forth. Had the early European invaders done this, they would soon have had to acknowledge that, not only did they have much to teach the Native Americans about God's Word, they also had much to learn.

That is not all, however. Suppose that we were to begin our theological work, not with the presupposition that we know nothing about God apart from the written Scriptures and the teachings we have received from Europe, but rather with the presupposition that God's Word has indeed been always with us. In that case, we give credence to what the Bible says, not because we have been told and therefore believe a priori that it is the Word of God, but rather because it resonates with and is authenticated by the Word that we have received through the generations. To some degree, that is what has already taken place, even though we do not often acknowledge it. As Cain Felder says with reference to the black experience:

> The Black Church and others within Black religious traditions give allegiance to biblical faith and witness, primarily because their own experiences seem to be depicted in the Bible. Many of the biblical stories reflect the existential reality of the "black story" for the last few centuries in an environment typically hostile to the interest of Blacks attaining their full sense of human potential. Blacks have become all too familiar with being oppressed by the socio-economic forces of political powers—foreign and domestic—arrayed against them. They have found in the Bible ancient symbols of their predicament, namely the saga of the Egyptian bondage, the

devastation of Assyrian Invasions, the deportation into Babylonian Captivity and the bedevilment by Principalities and Powers of the present age. Blacks have consequently developed an "experiential sympathy" with much of the Bible, which in turn receives reverent attention as quite literally the revealed Word of God.[21]

Womanist theologian Jacquelyn Grant agrees:

The God of the Old and New Testament became real in the consciousness of oppressed Black women. Though they were politically impotent, they were able to appropriate certain themes of the Bible which spoke to their reality. . . . An ex-slave woman revealed that when her experience negated certain oppressive interpretations of the Bible given by White preachers, she, through engaging the biblical message for herself, rejected them.[22]

It is possible to relate this to the traditional Methodist Quadrilateral, whose four elements are thus reinterpreted.[23]

First let us begin with the matter of experience. During the discussions at the Roundtable, we all seem to have agreed that experience is of great importance, but also that what we mean by "experience" must be understood in a much wider sense than is customary. Precisely because the Word of God is the light that enlightens everyone, experience must not be limited to Christian, or even to "religious" experience. If it is true that the Word who was incarnate is the same Word who was in the beginning, and through whom all things were made, all human experience must somehow be related to that Word. The Europeans did not bring the Word to the Western Hemisphere. That Word was here since creation, and that Word was the light that produced the values that were already here. When a Native American spoke of what later the Europeans called the "Great Spirit," this was spoken because of the Word that was incarnate in Christ and who speaks in Scripture. And when Africans or Koreans, even centuries before the arrival of the first missionary or the first slave trader, loved their children and sought to establish an orderly society, they did this by the same Word whom we have seen in Jesus Christ.

When the term "experience" is used in the context of Christian theology, what is usually meant is religious experience. If, however, the Word of God who became incarnate in Christ is the one through whom all things were made, and who enlightens everyone, it follows that all human experience must somehow relate to that Word. Not only is the experience of conversion, or of close communion with Christ, relevant to Christian theology. If the Quadrilateral is to be properly understood, the experience of slavery, which the African American community brings with itself, must also be seen as part of "experience." And the same must be said for all the concerns, pains, hopes, and frustrations each of us brings to the Christian roundtable.

Second this leads us to the matter of tradition. On this point, it is necessary first of all to widen our understanding of Christian tradition. For United Methodist Hispanics, for instance, it is important that the church understand that we belong to Christian tradition long before Wesley or the rise of the Anglo-Saxon powers. But tradition must also be understood in a much wider sense. If it is true that the Christ whom we worship and seek to serve is the Cosmic Word of God, it must also be true that in that sense all tradition, all history, is part of the history of redemption. There is no such thing as a history of redemption apart from the history of the world, and much less a history of redemption that is limited to the history of the church.

> The theology of incarnation requires that we view world history as an affirmative and positive salvific drama in which the people of God become responsible partners with God. . . . History, one in which we find our being and the only one which we will ever know, is the stage of God's salvific drama and the locus of *Heilsgeschichte*.[24]

I accept and affirm this with some difficulty, for I have spent most of my life being a historian of the church, and I still consider this to be my primary vocation. But I see the need for us to develop, not only ecclesiastical historians, but also Christian historians, people who are trained to see and to study the entire history of humankind as salvation history. How is the history of Japan, even before Francis Xavier or Commodore Perry, part of the history of salvation? That is the issue we must explore as we speak of tradition in the context of the Quadrilateral.

Third, the Quadrilateral speaks of reason. Here again, we must redefine what we mean by reason. Too often this has meant the detached and static reason of the Eleatic philosophical tradition, where changelessness is the mark of truth. What about reason understood in a more dynamic sense? On this point, Jung Young Lee called our attention to the possibility of a theology built on the paradigm of the yin-yang symbol, which represents a process of change, so that "it is not substance that changes, but it is change that creates substance and being."[25] He also indicated that on the basis of this paradigm it is possible to declare the logic of "either/or" to be insufficient, and to prefer to it the logic of "both/and," as being more capable of accounting for change and for the mutually inclusive polarity of yin and yang. Or, what about the "historical reason" or the "vital reason" of José Ortega y Gasset? What about reason as the wisdom of a people? What about the reason involved in the myths of origins, not only of the Hebrews, but also of the Cherokee or the Ibo? Can our use of "reason" in the Quadrilateral include these possibilities?[26]

Finally, we return to the fourth element in the Quadrilateral, which is also the main topic of this chapter: Scripture. What all of this means is that the authority of Scripture, like that of any of the other elements in the Quadrilateral, does not stand by itself. The authority of Scripture is related to and based on its relationship to the other three elements, and vice versa. It has often been argued by various traditional theologians that the church drew its canon because it recognized in the various books the gospel by which it lived. It must also be said that we accept the authority of Scripture in part because we recognize in it a Word that has also come to us in our corporate traditions, experience, and reason.

We are well aware that there are many who see matters differently, and that in recent years some in The United Methodist Church have backed away from the Quadrilateral, which they see as a concession to liberalism, and have tended to emphasize the primacy of Scripture. However, in our discussions many made clear that they disagreed with this trend on two counts: First, as I have already shown, it is possible to understand the Quadrilateral in a manner very different from that of the traditional middle-class white liberal. Second, as Ignacio Castuera stated during one of our discussions, "The emphasis on the primacy of Scripture most often reflects a white conservative tendency which is then strengthened by recruiting fundamentalist minorities, but whose true agenda is that the primacy belongs to *their reading* of Scripture." In other words, much of the emphasis on the primacy of Scripture we are seeing today is not willing to take into account the degree to which social, cultural, and other factors affect biblical interpretation, and therefore it takes for granted that the manner in which the dominant culture interprets Scripture is the only acceptable one.

Oddly enough, all of this does not mean that our discussion led in the direction of undermining the authority of Scripture, but rather in the direction of strengthening it, as the rest of this chapter will hopefully show.

TRADITIONAL CULTURES AND BIBLICAL FAITH

A theme that appeared repeatedly during the Roundtable's discussions on hermeneutics, was the many parallels between the world view of the Bible and those of traditional cultures.[27] In this respect, there are many contrasts between the experience and theology of the dominant culture, on the one hand, and those of ethnic minorities, on the other.

The mainstream of Western North-Atlantic theology has found it increasingly necessary, especially during the last three centuries, to build bridges between the "modern" Western world and the Bible. It was a time when Western civilization and culture were rapidly evolving, and through that evolution the North-Atlantic tribe was attaining hegemony over the rest of the world. The resulting imperial expansion of the West—politically as well as economically and culturally—certainly influenced other cultures. Much has been written about that. But the expansion also influenced Western culture, eroding many of its values and destroying its traditional views of the world. The "modern" world view is so prevalent, and so successful in its manipulation and exploitation of the natural world, that in many circles it currently passes for the only rational or reasonable understanding of the world. The net result in theology, and particularly in biblical interpretation, has been the need to demythologize, as Bultmann correctly pointed out—or perhaps better, to remythologize into the myth patterns of the twentieth-century Western technocratic myth system. Passages in the Bible dealing with miracles, demons, and divine intervention in human and natural affairs, many of which have been sources of strength for believers throughout the centuries, have become the most problematic for many in the dominant culture—and, precisely because of the dominant power of that culture, for many in other cultures.

It should be said in passing that this is not the only possible world view. Even today, it is not the world view of the vast majority of humankind. Nor is its logic so "objective" and purely rational as is often claimed. As I have pointed out elsewhere, ever since Kant, and especially after Marx and Freud, we have known that "reason" is highly influenced by subconscious processes of which we are often not aware. On that basis,

> One could argue that the view that the universe is closed and its workings are like those of a machine is part of the ideology by which those who control the present order destroy or curtail the hope of those whose only hope lies in change. "Modern reason" precludes our thinking in terms of divine intervention. But by whose standards of "modernity" and whose definition of "reason"? [28]

A similar argument can be made with reference to the sort of biblical scholarship that has gone hand-in-hand with such "modernity." Making use of the work of Vincent Wimbush, Cain Felder reminded the Roundtable that "the 'high' Protestant adoption of critical analysis of the biblical text was a by-product of the new consciousness among the literate bourgeois classes of Europe and America." [29] And white biblical scholar Norman Gottwald agrees:

Biblical scholars from the Renaissance to the bourgeois revolutions of the seventeenth through the nineteenth centuries were generally the intellectual adjuncts of monarchic, aristocratic, or clerical class interests. Increasingly in the nineteenth century, they became one functional group among many academicians and intellectuals who shared in the bourgeois revolutions against monarchic and aristocratic domination. . . . By and large the position of biblical scholars, as a professional and intellectual elite, was oppositional both toward the declining monarchies and aristocracies and toward the rising underclasses of the industrial proletariat and, later, the peasantry.[30]

From the perspective of such scholarship, and of the many theologians and pastors who have been trained under its aegis, most ethnic minority churches are dominated by "fundamentalism." A common experience of black, Native American, Latino, and Asian American seminary students in mostly white "mainline" seminaries is that even before they express their views, and much more thereafter, they are dubbed "fundamentalists" by their white professors and peers. This is understandable, since they often speak of the Bible and of its world view—demons and all—in a way that is similar to that of the fundamentalists.

At this point, however, some clarifications must be made. It is necessary to remember that fundamentalism is in its origin essentially a white North American movement, a reaction against the "modern" world view and biblical scholarship that I have just described. Although the term "fundamentals" had been circulating for some time, it was in 1895, at Niagara Falls, that "fundamentalism" proper was born. It was there that the five "fundamentals" that gave the movement its name were listed and affirmed: the inerrancy of Scripture, the divinity of Jesus, the Virgin birth, the work of Jesus at the cross as a substitutionary payment for our sins, and his physical resurrection and impending return. Interestingly enough, as is the case with every reactionary movement, fundamentalism limited its list to those elements it saw threatened, and did not have a word to say about the Holy Spirit, salvation, ethics, or a host of other subjects crucial to biblical faith.

Fundamentalism is by nature and by origin reactionary—a response to a perceived threat. As such, it can arise and exist only where "modernism"—whatever that may mean—is also present. Therefore, an apparently simple, traditional, even "naive" understanding of Scripture is not the same as fundamentalism. When an African American congregation sings, "Didn't my Lord deliver Daniel?" it is not reacting to liberal ideas, which would deny the historicity of Daniel. That is not the point. What the congregation is making is a profound statement of its own identity and its dependence on the God who delivered Daniel. (Which, by the way, is probably closer to the purpose of the author than is either a liberal or a fundamentalist reading of the text, both of which get bogged down on the question of historicity, and have great difficulties reaching the question of meaning.)

The same may be said of the manner in which other minority and Third World groups read the Bible.

> Dr. Hseng-Chu Wang, professor of theology at Tainan Theological Seminary in Taiwan, recently stated that most European-American theologians treat the Old Testament as the "interesting history" of the Hebrews. The Taiwanese, however, view the Old Testament very differently. Living under domination of foreign power for four centuries, their history destroyed, their identity as a people diffused by colonization, the Old Testament is their story. The identification of their struggle with the struggle of the Israelites moving toward the promised land is very clear. This can be said of any oppressed community—be it Third World countries, the southern hemisphere, ethnic minorities or women in the United States.[31]

In this respect, fundamentalism differs radically from the traditional acceptance and use of the Bible by ethnic minority groups. Fundamentalism takes as its starting point the authority of Scripture, quite apart—at least in theory—from the degree to which it resonates with the experience and culture of the community. If there is dissonance, it is the experience and the culture that must be wrong and must be adjusted to the Bible. Hence the Scopes trial and scientific creationism. The ethnic minority community, on the other hand, grants authority to Scripture precisely because Scripture resonates with the culture and experience of the group. I have already quoted Cain Felder, to the effect that the reason why the African American community grants such authority to Scripture is that it sees itself in the biblical text. The story of Moses is important to the black community, not primarily because it is in the Bible, but because that community can find itself in the story. Likewise, when the first missionaries went to Asia with the Bible, that book was granted authority, not because it was considered a priori to be the Word of God, but because it resonated with the experiences of Asian converts. In Latin America, which is traditionally Roman Catholic, and where the Bible was not in the hands of the general population until the arrival of Protestantism, something similar took place—although in this case there was already the sense that the Bible, though unknown, was authoritative. People read the Bible and found that it spoke to their situation and their experience. The resultant reading of Scripture could be considered "naive" or even "primitive"—words that do not necessarily have the pejorative connotation modern Western society has given them; but they are not the same as fundamentalism.

There are many examples that could be given of such apparently naive, but in truth profound, interpretation of Scripture. This is what the African American tradition has been doing all along as its songs have insisted on the parting of the Red Sea as the crucial saving act of God in the Hebrew Scriptures—a point on which modern scholars have eventually come to agree with the African American community. This is what is being done every day in thousands of places across this entire hemisphere, where poor and oppressed people gather to read the Bible, not to find in it what others have always found, but truly to seek guidance for their lives as individuals and as communities.[32] Thus, in an immigrant community, when the story of Pentecost is heard, a refugee who has great difficulty with English says, "They heard, each in their own tongue. The Spirit didn't expect them all to learn the language. The Spirit translated, because all languages are equally important." And, in a Korean American community, a woman suddenly exclaims, "Mary chose the better part. She was supposed to stay in the kitchen, like Martha. But she did not. She came out to where the men were supposed to be. And Jesus said it was better than to stay in the kitchen!" Such interpretations may be unsophisticated, but they are not fundamentalism. They are born out of the conviction that Scripture has something to say to us today, not out of a drive to make certain that Scripture says over and over again what it has always said to other generations in other places.

This is not to say that fundamentalism has not made significant inroads into the ethnic minority community. What Homer Noley says about Native Americans is true for all of our communities: "Most Native American clergy are schooled in non-Indian Christianity, and therefore reflect the fundamentalism of rural white America."[33] When missionaries went to Latin America or to Asia, the "liberals" found the native world views so alien that they did not know how to relate to them, while the fundamentalists found it easier to equate their interpretation of Scripture with the manner in which their converts interpreted it. Likewise, in the case of the African American community, liberals found it possible to join hands with blacks on some of the civil rights agenda; but they looked down with condescension on much black biblical interpretation. Furthermore, since the printed media usually represent the concerns and perspectives of the dominant culture, only two theological alternatives were made available in print: fundamentalism and liberalism. Given such circumstances, and the almost total lack of understanding of ethnic minority churches on the part of the ecclesiastical and theological establishment, it is not surprising that true fundamentalism, though in essence alien to the minority community, has made significant inroads into it.

A further factor, however, is much more important. It may be that, from the perspective of the majority church, the point at which the ethnic minority churches are closest to the biblical world view is the matter of miracles and the like; but from the ethnic minority perspective there are other matters far more important. Foremost among these is a holistic approach. Western civilization, at least since the time of the Renaissance and in many respects even before that, has tended to separate the religious from the secular. In contrast, the various cultures we represent have mostly held the opposite view. In the case of Native Americans, Homer Noley (Choctaw) points out that

> European peoples appeared to believe that religion was something that operated within society alongside political theories and philosophical systems. For Native American tribes, spiritual traditions were the totality of their tribal systems. While to Europeans religion was optional within a society, to individual Native American tribes their spiritual traditions provided the basis for community order and societal well being.[34]

The distancing between the secular and the religious is thoroughly unbiblical, and is also foreign to the traditional cultures represented in ethnic minority churches. Yet it serves an ideological function, particularly when the religious is identified with the private, and most social, political, and economic matters are then relegated to the realm of the secular. This point is often made, both by ethnic minority theologians and by whites who are aware of the manner in which traditional theology has been used to justify the status quo, or at least to prevent religion from challenging it. In his paper on hermeneutics, Stephen Kim expressed it in terms that found support among others at the Roundtable:

> Western theology in the nineteenth and twentieth centuries has devoted itself primarily to personal/moral issues over those that are social, political, and cultural. And it has been so, owing to its compatibility, or desire for compatibility, with temporal powers.[35]

It is at this point that traditional Western theology has proved most insidious to ethnic minority communities. As just stated, the traditional culture of such communities is one in which there is a continuum between the secular and the religious, so that religious matters are closely entwined with the manner in which community life is organized and its resources are distributed. By introducing into such communities the non-biblical distinction between the secular and the religious, traditional Western Christian theology has contributed significantly to the disempowerment of minorities, and to the dismemberment of their cultures. Such theology has been used to convince the powerless that issues of power and its use are secular, and therefore have nothing to do with their religion or with the will of God. As a by-product, this distinction has also resulted in schizoid tensions within ethnic minority Christianity, where many have accepted it as biblical and essentially Christian, because they were so taught, and yet remain sufficiently close to their traditional culture that they find the distinction itself unnatural and even unbearable.

This is perhaps the main reason why many ethnic minority theologians are insisting on the point made earlier, namely, that the authority of Scripture does not stand alone, but is closely related to, and grounded on, the manner in which the Bible resonates with our culture and experience, so that we find in Scripture the same Word of God that has been revealed to us and to our ancestors throughout the generations. Most of us are willing to concede that the Bible has a corrective function vis-à-vis our traditional culture and beliefs. Yet, we must insist that this corrective function be found by ourselves, as we read Scripture from the perspective of our own cultural heritage, and not dictated by others from outside—others, let it be stated plainly, who are often not as ready to apply the corrective message of Scripture to their own culture and traditions as radically as they wish to apply it to ours. What Felder, following indications of several African scholars, says about African theology today is also true about much ethnic minority theology in this country: They "are *presupposing* the legitimacy of their traditional world-view, but interrogating the Bible and its Western interpreters regarding *their* legitimacy among Africans."[36]

The net result is not, as white North-Atlantic critics might expect, a lessening of the authority of Scripture, but is rather greater respect for such authority, which is soon seen not to depend on the mediation of Western culture, Greek modes of thought, and so forth, but on the contrary, to be closely related to our traditional cultures and values.

IN QUEST OF A HERMENEUTICS OF COMMUNITY

A further theme that appeared in every one of the presentations on hermeneutics, as well as in our entire discussion, was the need for community, not merely as a support for the individual, but rather as the proper locus for the hermeneutical task. In my own paper, I did not deal extensively with that subject, mostly because elsewhere, and at the same time, I had written a plea for what I have called "Fuenteovejuna theology,"[37] meaning by that a theology undertaken with such a sense of community that it belongs to the community itself, and at the end no one knows who first proposed a particular idea. This obviously stands in sharp contrast with the "normal" way of engaging in theology in the dominant culture, and particularly in academic circles, where people often dispute as to who originated a particular idea.

Such private ownership of ideas is alien to the cultural background of most ethnic minorities, even though most of us have become so acculturated to the North-Atlantic individualistic ideology that we no longer find the notion of owning an idea so bizarre as it really is. In most traditional cultures, an idea belongs to the community, not to the individual who somehow was the channel employed by the spiritual powers to communicate the idea to the community. In early Christian theology, the same is true: Ideas come from the eternal Logos or Word of God, and to claim them for ourselves is to usurp what belongs to God. (It may be said in passing that the same is true about the private ownership of land, which most traditional cultures would find irrational,[38] and the Bible finds objectionable,[39] and yet we have come to consider absolutely normal and even normative.)

It was Stephen S. Kim's paper which most emphasized the significance of community as a hermeneutical tool and goal. This may be seen in the very title of his paper: "From I-Hermeneutics to We-Hermeneutics: Prolegomenon to Theology of Community from an Asian-American Perspective."[40] What Dr. Kim argues in this paper goes far beyond the proposal that Scripture is best understood within the circumstances of a community, and when interpreted by a community. He would certainly affirm that, but he places it within the larger framework of a theology in which the notion of community stands at the very center.

According to Dr. Kim, both the West and the East have traditionally sought the meaning of existence in the "I-consciousness." This, however, is not where such meaning is to be found, at least according to the gospel of Jesus Christ. "We believe that the realization of the Kingdom of God, 'an authentic community,' is God's will and the essence of the Gospel."[41] Thus, community is not just a hermeneutical tool and a necessary context in which to understand a text, but also the goal of every interpretation and every text to be interpreted. Without such a perspective and goal, we fall into I-hermeneutics, which fails, not merely because it misinterprets its text, but also because it misinterprets its task. The task of hermeneutics is not merely for an individual—or even for a community—to understand a text, but is even more for building the community, which is God's purpose for creation.

Although it is common and quite natural for ethnic minorities to create a sense of community around their ethnicity, Kim is quite clear that the community to which he is referring, while including the contributions and concerns of all ethnic groups, is not to be interpreted in ethnic terms. "WE is not simply a WE as opposed to YOU, but WE which represents all human beings."[42] This is the central meaning of the gospel.

We also believe that the ultimate purpose of Jesus Christ's mission and ministry as manifested in his life, death, and resurrection was to realize such authentic community in which all creation was redeemed and liberated from sin and oppression. "All creation" here must be interpreted to include everybody in need of redemption, liberation, and salvation, not just "minjung," not just Koreans or ethnic minorities, but all who need redemption and liberation. "Liberation" must also be understood to mean more than social, economical, and political; it must also include ethical and spiritual liberation. This, I believe, was the intention of Jesus when he taught about the Kingdom of God. An authentic community, by its definition, must not overlook any member of the human community, however insignificant and however undeserving. There was no undeserving soul as far as Jesus was concerned. He could not and would not close the door of the Kingdom on one lost sheep.[43]

For this reason, Kim suggests that we must redefine growth in Christian discipleship in terms that are less individualistic and more communal. Using an image that has become quite common in English-speaking Christianity, he redefines the image of the Pilgrim's Progress, which has so often been understood in the sense of personal improvement. For him, the progress of the Christian pilgrim in truth refers "to the journey from the reclusive, escapist, egotistic immature faith toward the Christian maturity which takes joy in the participatory, sacrificial, compassionate life."[44]

It is in this respect that "the immigrant church" has a particular role, and that we must clarify the significance and content of what Kim calls "an immigrant theology." Having come to "this our new adopted homeland," and found the United States an already existing concept of community, one that does not include us, part of our task is precisely to widen that concept of community. This is to be done, not only for our sake, but also and above all for the sake of the entire community, which otherwise is truncated and falsified.

Those who have come before us think they have already built theirs [i.e., their authentic community], but it does not suit us and does not meet our needs; our vision is a larger and more authentic one; ours is that the new community is for all, not just the ones we want and need, but all whom God has chosen, and to whom God's open invitation is extended.[45]

It is on the basis of this perspective that Kim then goes on to study and interpret the parable of the laborers (Matt. 20:1-16). What he suggests is that the interpretation of a parable such as this requires a new logic, for "the more logically and reasonably one wants to interpret this parable, the more injustice one feels has been committed by the employer in the story."[46] He suggests in passing that a parable such as this is much more difficult to understand by those "who have been taught to expect a more perfect state of things" than by those who "from the very earliest times in our life, became accustomed to unnatural ways of life, a life that has seen contradictions and irrationality."[47] Or, as others would say, there is a "hermeneutical privilege" on the part of the oppressed.[48] Kim's conclusion is that "a call to community . . . is the core of the parable, even beyond the lesson of service." What is offered here is "a vision of an authentic community in which every individual's worth is respected in a fuller way than it is possible to explain and justify rationally and legalistically." And this in turn has direct implications for immigrant theology: "Immigrants, in other words, have as much claim and stake in discipleship and community as the early settlers."[49]

Such a call for community, both as the framework and as the goal of the hermeneutical task, found general support among those at the Roundtable. Yet, profound dissatisfaction was also expressed: Although we "talk a good game" we still have not truly devised methodologies that give full expression to that centrality of community. In her response to Kim's paper, Naomi Southard paraphrased the title of an essay by black writer Audre Lorde, "One cannot use the master's tools to dismantle the master's house." By this she meant, in part, that the very process we followed at the Roundtable, of presenting papers and commenting on them, was so tainted by the individualistic and academic setting of white theology, that the very call for community was contradicted. On this point, she declared: "I long for the time and the place when we can address the doing of theology which is both in format and content, more community-oriented."[50] She also added a significant dimension, which was then taken up and affirmed by her colleagues, namely, that the parable not only calls for community, but also speaks to the new order in that community, for it "challenges the basic assumption of the patriarchal system which supports the hierarchical structure of society—that domination/subordination, have/have-not, rich/poor are acceptable and can be justified."[51] And she forced the entire Roundtable to greater sobriety on the theme of community, reminding us that, while "individualist-oriented" persons and groups have serious shortcomings, "collectivist-oriented" ones have their own—the most glaring among them being the tendency to limit sharing to members of the same group.[52] Along the same lines, it was clear to us that, if the community of which Dr. Kim spoke is to come about, this will require radical conversion, so that those who oppress others will cease their oppression, and those who are oppressed will reclaim their dignity.

These last points are of crucial importance as ethnic minorities devise their own theologies, for the theme of "community" is a two-edged sword. On the one hand, because the community at large seldom has a place for us, we do tend to have a greater and more conscious sense of the need for community. On the other hand, and precisely for the same reason, we are always tempted to create an ethnic community over against the dominant community and its racism. Although such ethnic communities are important for matters of identity, and may be necessary in order to gain a modicum of justice in situations in which the dominant community excludes ethnic minorities, they are a poor substitute for the all-inclusive community envisioned in Kim's paper. To this we shall return in the chapter dealing with the church.

TRANSLATION AND INTERPRETATION

The multiple witness of Scripture, which was discussed in the foregoing chapter, is what makes it possible and even advisable to translate the Bible. Quite clearly, every translation is also an interpretation. Languages do not correspond neatly to one another, so that one can translate by simply substituting one word for another. At every turn, it is necessary to choose among many possible alternatives. How does one translate "nice" into German? How does one translate "simpático" into English? Much depends on the perspective and the choice of the translator. It is for that reason that we often and quite accurately refer to a translator as an "interpreter." For the same reason, the Italians have a saying, *tradutore traditore*—a translator is a traitor. No translation can convey the exact meaning of the original, without accretions, diminutions, and various nuances introduced by the translation itself.[53]

If it is true that every translation is also an interpretation, the question immediately arises, How can a translation be authoritative? One possible answer is to claim a miraculous intervention in the process of translation itself. When this question was posed to the Greek-speaking Jews of Alexandria regarding their Greek Bible, they had recourse to an elaborate legend. According to that legend, seventy-two elders were commissioned with the task of translating the Hebrew Scriptures into Greek. They worked independently of one another. Yet, when their translations were compared, they were found to be identical. Clearly, the purpose of this legend is to bolster the authority of the Greek translation—which derives its name, "Septuagint," from the legend itself. But the theological framework of the legend, and the understanding of revelation that lies behind it, are quite foreign to what lies behind the quadriform witness to the gospel and the variety of perspectives in the whole of Scripture. Indeed, the reason why this legend was necessary was that the Greek-speaking community in Alexandria came to see the Hebrew Scriptures, not as the history of what God had done, and the promises of what God would do, for Israel, but rather as something similar to a Greek oracle.[54] In a Greek oracle, what is important are the words, rather than the events behind them. The revelation is in the words, even though at times they do not even make sense. If such is the case with Scripture, then it is imperative that the words be authoritative, and also that, in the case of a translation, that translation be certified to be equally as authoritative as the original.

A corollary of such an understanding is that there can only be one authoritative translation.[55] In a way, this understanding of the inspiration of Scripture stands behind the decision of the Council of Trent that the books of the Bible were to be read "as they are contained in the old Latin Vulgate Edition."[56] The practical reason for this decision was that various Protestant leaders had produced translations from Hebrew and Greek into the vernaculars of Europe, and on a number of issues such translations disagreed with the Vulgate and with doctrines that had been based on it. At a deeper level, however, what was at stake was an understanding of scriptural revelation and of catholicity. During the Middle Ages, the church had grown accustomed to interpreting the Bible as if it were a Greek oracle. Phrases taken out of context were said to be divine revelation, because they were found in Scripture, and then employed as theological arguments. The resultant theology, which owed much to the particular social and cultural circumstances of medieval Western Europe, was then considered the only possible theology, and given the name "catholic," even though in reality it was far from being such. Thus, the insistence on a single authoritative translation is part and parcel of an entire theological outlook—one that stands in sharp contradiction with the fourfold witness to the gospel in the New Testament.

Nor is this a problem only among Tridentine Roman Catholics. Similar views of revelation lie behind discussions among some fundamentalist Protestants regarding whether humans are composed of body, soul, and spirit, or only of body and soul. In such discussions, the Bible is read as if it were an oracle. The "trichotomists" find a text that speaks of "spirit, soul, and body," and on the basis of that text stand ready to wage theological war on the "dichotomists," who find a different formula in other texts. Even apart from the question of the relevance of the issue, one wonders how such theological methodology can take account of the fourfold witness to the gospel. Indeed, the main difficulty with fundamentalism is not, as some claim, that it is out of touch with the modern world, but rather that it is out of touch with Scripture, which if taken seriously does not allow itself to be read as an oracle.[57]

How, then, can a translation be authoritative? One possible answer is to claim that a particular translation, for whatever reason, is not human interpretation, but is rather the result of a special divine intervention, à la Septuagint. This, however, is to deny the very nature of Scripture, as is seen in the fourfold witness to the gospel and in all the other instances that have been mentioned here.

A better answer is to acknowledge that Scripture itself is interpretation, and that therefore to interpret Scripture is not to deny its authority, but to acknowledge its particular kind of authority. We often say that "Scripture is its best interpreter." That is true; but we must clarify what it means. It does not mean that the Bible is a divine oracle, fallen from heaven, so that each word has a mystical significance, if only we can discover it in other parts of Scripture. Such was the approach of Origen, the great Alexandrian teacher of the third century, who came to the conclusion that in the Bible "cloud" means "voice," "horse" means "strength," and so on. He then proceeded to reread the entirety of Scripture discovering in it supposedly hidden meanings.

When we say that the Bible is its best interpreter, what we mean is that in the Bible itself one sees the interpretation and reinterpretation of an event. The Bible is its best interpreter because it is its first interpreter. Thus the flight from Egypt and the wandering in the wilderness becomes in Second-Isaiah the prototype for the return from exile, and in I Corinthians and I Peter the prototype for Christian baptism and the Christian life. This point was clearly made by Ediberto López at the Roundtable of 1989, commenting on Severino Croatto's hermeneutical theory: "In the Bible the memory of an event is gathered, but is never a repetition of the original meaning, but rather an exploration of its reserve of meaning."[58] The Bible is its best interpreter because it refuses to take itself as an oracle from heaven, and in so doing sets the pattern for every other biblical interpretation.

It is within this situation and from this perspective that ethnic minority theologies find a place and a contribution. The Bible we have received is already a translation, and this in a sense that far surpasses the obvious fact of linguistic translation. We have received it through the mediation of centuries of interpretation, mostly within the setting of Western civilization, and even within the narrower setting of the Germanic and Anglo-Saxon portion of that civilization. When we read the Bible, no matter whether it is in English or in one of our many native languages, we tend to read it as we were taught, that is to say, in what amounts to a white, Western, Anglo-Saxon translation. To the degree that we allow ourselves to do so, we lose the opportunity to hear Scripture as it speaks to us today, in our culture and situation, and the church at large loses whatever insights into the meaning of the gospel we might have been able to contribute. When, on the other hand, we look again at the Bible, and read it afresh from the perspective of our own cultures and within the circumstances of our own situations, we discover new meanings, which are a contribution to the whole church catholic.

These meanings, in contrast to much that we have received as standard biblical interpretation, are profoundly and freshly liberating, as the examples given in this chapter amply show.

That is the sort of contribution that we who are participants in the Ethnic Theologians' Roundtable hope to make, and to encourage others to make.

CHAPTER FOUR

VISIONS OF THE WORLD

CREATION AND REDEMPTION

Although standard treatises on systematic theology usually deal first with the doctrine of God, then with creation, and much later with salvation, there is a question as to whether theology should be creation-centered, or redemption-centered. Many would argue that, although beginning with creation may make sense in terms of a logical outline, or of the order of being, the experience of salvation precedes the doctrine of creation in the order of knowledge. As Ignacio Castuera pointed out in one of the sessions of the Roundtable, "The biblical God was first experienced as a liberating God who cared deeply for Israel," and then as the creator God. "The people of Israel first came to know the love of God, *then* scavenged around and came up with a mix from other sources."[1] Such an approach, which Castuera relates to Hispanic experience, finds parallels in African American experience, as is indicated by Ed Wimberly:

> Exodus is the central story that interprets other stories for Afro-Americans. Therefore, Exodus becomes the central image used for understanding the two creation stories of Genesis I, II, and III. Some theologians take Genesis I to be the central story of creation because of its emphasis on the goodness of creation without any blemishes. However, other theologians would focus on Genesis II and III as the central image of creation, with human finiteness and human flaws as central. However, Exodus as the central story has helped Afro-Americans to affirm the goodness of God's creation, and at the same time it has helped them to see human frailty in themselves as well as in their oppressors. Therefore, Exodus has helped Afro-Americans embrace the complexity of life—creation and creators as good while possessing flaws that need redeeming.[2]

To this, Wimberly adds another dimension with which Castuera would also agree: "Exodus makes sense to Afro-American Christians because

Christ redeems and liberates. Therefore, Jesus Christ is the central figure that has enabled Afro-Americans to appropriate the Exodus story."[3]

That the experience of salvation-liberation is prior to the doctrine of creation, finds support in what we know of the history of Israel and the formation of its sacred scripture. Although Christians have traditionally thought otherwise, the main theme of the Pentateuch is not creation, but the Exodus and the manner in which the people who have experienced such a mighty saving act of God are to order their lives. In the Pentateuch, creation is a prelude to the central theme of redemption. Furthermore, it is the story of the Exodus and the surrounding events that gives the Pentateuch—as well as the entire Hebrew Scriptures—its particular character. As Castuera aptly put it, the people of Israel "scavenged around" for stories of creation that would depict the creative activity of the God whom they knew as their redeemer from the yoke of Egypt. In that process, they took up stories of creation and other myths of origins, adapted them to their purposes, so that the God depicted in them would not be the multitudinous and capricious gods in the original versions, and out of them made a foreword to the election of Abraham and the deliverance from Egypt.

This, which modern biblical scholars tell us and such ethnic theologians as Castuera and Wimberly affirm, is also confirmed by the experience of many a Christian. For such Christians, conversion is not usually to the creator God, but rather to the redeemer God, who then is also experienced as creator and ruler of the world around us. One moves from the experience of alienation, brokenness, and captivity, to redemption, wholeness, and liberation, and then to creation, for without such experiences the world is not perceived as the creation of a good God.

Although there is a positive aspect to this approach, the problem is that, in this view, Genesis 3 is often more important than Genesis 1 and 2. Creation has been corrupted by the "Fall," which is now the dominant sign under which we all live. There is much in the history of Israel and of Western Christianity that has served to reinforce this emphasis on the Fall and its consequences. In the history of Israel, being a small nation at the very crossroads where several successive mighty empires met did not lead to a sense of peace with the world. Captivity in Egypt; subjection to neighboring peoples; exile in Babylon; humiliation and cultural imperialism on the part of Hellenistic Syria; conquest by Rome—these were but a few of the many painful episodes in which Israel experienced alienation and despair. Thus, one should not be surprised to find expressions of deep alienation in such a Jew as Paul of Tarsus:

> But I am of the flesh, sold into slavery under sin. I do not understand my own actions. For I do not do what I want, but I do the very thing I hate. Now if I do what I do not want, I agree that the law is good. But in fact it is no

longer I that do it, but sin that dwells within me. For I know that nothing good dwells within me, that is, in my flesh. I can will what is right, but I cannot do it. For I do not do the good I want, but the evil I do not want is what I do. Now if I do what I do not want, it is no longer I that do it, but sin that dwells within me. (Rom. 7:14-20)

Building on this foundation, Western Christianity soon came to see sin and the Fall as the dominant sign under which all must live. In this respect, no single theologian was as influential as Augustine. If there is a word that characterizes the mood of the early portions of Augustine's *Confessions,* it is alienation. He is alienated from himself, whom he sees as a despicable sinner from childhood—among other things, for having stolen some green pears for the pure pleasure of the mischief. He is alienated from his father, of whom apparently he prefers not to speak. He is alienated from his mother, and cannot forgive himself for it. He is ashamed of his sexuality, and yet cannot control it. He spends years of connubial life with a woman, and then dismisses her, under pressure from his mother, without even mentioning her name. For such a "sinner," the experience at the garden in Milan, and the ensuing reconciliation with his mother, is formative. It is through that lens that he will always interpret, not only his own life, but all of human existence.

It was out of that experience of alienation and reconciliation that Augustine devised his understanding of grace, which we would find strange, were we not so shaped by it. Augustine, the great Doctor of Grace, has a very ungracious attitude toward grace. Grace is God's love acting for our salvation. So far so good. But grace is also an irresistible power, granted to some and denied to others by a God who predestines a specific number in order to fill the gap left by the fallen angels. The rest, because of original sin, are nothing but a "mass of damnation."

As if Augustine's experience of inner alienation were not enough, at the end of his life his world collapsed into political alienation. His native Africa was invaded by the Vandals, Germanic hordes that had crossed over from Europe. The rest of the Western Roman Empire suffered a similar fate. Woeful times ensued. Life became cheap, and death common. While many forgot Augustine's doctrine of the free and unmerited grace of God, his doctrine of sin reigned supreme. The loving Creator God faded into the background, obscured by a harsh God who kept accounts of sin, judged all, and forgave little. Hell was described in ever more realistic terms. By contrast, heaven was dull and boring, and its main attraction was that it was an alternative to hell. For those who had not yet done enough to please this "Redeemer" God, there was purgatory, where they would suffer for centuries, until they had been purged of their sin. For little ones, who died without actual sin, but also without having been baptized, there was limbo.

Then came the Protestant Reformation, led by a friar whose alienation from God was such that he later commented: "I did not love, yes, I hated the righteous God who punishes sinners, and secretly, if not blasphemously, certainly murmuring greatly, I was angry with God."[4] For Luther, there is a clear contrast between two ways of knowing God, resulting in what he calls the general and the particular knowledge of God. The first is related both with creation and with the existence and justice of God; the latter, with salvation.[5] What is important to know is not that God has made the universe, but that God is "for me." Thus, while chronologically it may be true that the knowledge of God as Creator is prior to the knowledge of God as Redeemer, existentially it is the latter that holds supreme importance.

And it was not only Luther who felt thus. Soon the supposedly best exponents of Protestant theology were speaking of "total depravity," "limited atonement," and "double predestination," and claiming that such ungracious doctrines were the best possible way to speak of the grace of God!

The result of this long history is that Christianity has been turned into a religion of salvation, much like the mysteries and the Gnosticism against which it struggled in its early centuries. In this state of affairs, "salvation" tends to lose the wide scope it has in Scripture, and to become salvation from fallenness and from a fallen world. In order to induce people to accept such salvation, it is necessary first of all to convince them that they are hopelessly lost. Indeed, the more lost they are, the more likely they will be to accept salvation. Hence a typical "evangelistic" sermon is one in which the starting point of the "good news" is that we are bound directly to hell, where we shall roast for an eternity. Such is the result of a religion whose real starting point is Genesis 3, and which interprets both creation and redemption from the perspective of the Fall.

It is not only fire-and-brimstone fundamentalists who have embraced such a theological outlook, which essentially denies the goodness of creation—at least as experienced by us this side of the Fall. Karl Barth would certainly disagree with the typical "evangelistic" sermon. His point of disagreement however, would not be that such preaching is too harsh, but rather that it is not harsh enough. The consequences of the Fall are such, and the corruption of our nature so profound, that we are unable even to recognize our own sin. One does not really know what sin is until one knows redemption. The impact of the Fall is such a crucial issue for Barth, that it is at this point that he sees one of the basic contrasts between Catholics and true Protestants. The latter cannot accept the Thomistic dictum, *gratia non tollit naturam, sed perficit*—grace does not destroy nature, but rather perfects it. Such a dictum seems to make light of the Fall and of the ensuing distance between nature and grace, between creation as it now exists and redemption. The Fall is so great, our depravity so total, that salvation can no longer be understood in terms of the perfection of created nature. Indeed, when some objected that even Calvin had some very good things to say about human nature, Barth and his followers responded that Calvin could only say such things under the heading "had Adam not fallen," and that therefore, this side of the Fall, all this is no longer true.

ANOTHER OPTION

It should be noted that the priority of redemption over creation results from a particular experience and world view, which is not necessarily shared by all. For instance, it was clear in our Roundtable deliberations that several Native American participants disagreed and would rather begin with an affirmation of the world and its wholeness. They would agree with the statement:

> Our ancestors had a relationship with God as Creator that was healthy and responsible long before they knew about Jesus. They had a relationship with [the] Creator that was solidified in the stories they told around the camp fires in each of our tribes, in their prayers, and especially in their ceremonies. This relationship began with the recognition of God as Creator, the creative force behind all things that exist, and long predated the coming of the missionaries. In that relationship, the people saw themselves as participants within creation as a whole, as a part of creation, and they celebrated the balance and harmony of the whole of the universe in all that they did together.[6]

Clearly, what we have here is much more than the question of whether to begin with creation or with redemption. It is not just a matter of where to start. It is also and above all a matter that has to do with the basic perspective one has on life and on the gospel. Native American critics of traditional Western theology have stated that "there are different places to start for any group of people to create a theology. . . . Many of America's churches use original sin as the starting point."[7] This has certainly affected our understanding of creation, so that Vine Deloria correctly describes the majority of Christians when he declares that "for the Christian it would appear that the importance of the creation event is that it sets the scene for an understanding of the entrance of sin into the world."[8]

The "Fall," however, is not the only starting point possible. Traditional Western theology is based on a hermeneutic that places Genesis 3 at its very heart, and then interprets everything accordingly. This is essentially a hermeneutic of alienation, one that so emphasizes the Fall that creation tends to fade into the background, as relating to an idyllic world which no longer exists. Again, we would do well to listen to what Native Americans tell us, for they may help us discover much, not only about ourselves, but also about the biblical message.

> Native Americans, Christian and traditional, still live out of their theology of creation, while immigrant Christians have long displaced creation from the center of theology in favor of an over-emphasis on a theology of redemption.[9]

The sense of alienation from creation which traditional Western theology derives from this emphasis on the Fall affects, not only the manner in which we read all of Scripture after Genesis 3, but even the manner in which we read the creation stories themselves, for we tend to project that alienation back to them.

Take one example. When Scripture tells us that God formed the first man out of the dust of the earth, and then blew on him, we tend to think that somehow the human predicament is related to our being made out of dirt. Indeed, there is a long tradition of interpretation, both at the level of erudite theology and at the level of popular religiosity, which sees matters thus. Our problem is that we are material beings into which God has blown the breath of life. But that is not at all what Scripture says. According to Scripture, our being made out of dirt is part of God's *good* creation. There is nothing wrong with being made out of dirt. On the contrary, it was God's intent from the beginning, and is still God's intent, that we be tied to the earth, as it were, by an umbilical cord. In Navajo culture, this sense of being tied to the earth is symbolized by the custom of burying the umbilical cord, so that the child will always remember its ties to the earth. Because we are made out of dirt, we are one creature among many, depending for our very lives on those other creatures, and on that very dirt from which we have sprung. In the famous words after the Fall, "Dust you are, and to dust you will return," the second part may be a curse resulting from sin; but the first part is a simple statement of a fact that was and is the result of God's creative action.

Likewise, when in the other creation story we are told that God said, "Let us make humankind in our image, according to our likeness; and let them have dominion over the fish of the sea, . . . and over every creeping thing that creeps upon the earth" (Gen. 1:26), Western theology and civilization have understood this to mean that the human creature stands above creation, and that "dominion" is a sort of carte blanche for the management of the rest of the created order. The result has been the destruction of much of nature, as well as the alienation of the human creature from the rest of creation.

> The second aspect of the Christian doctrine of creation that concerns us vitally today is the idea that man receives dominion over the rest of creation. . . . It is this attitude that has been adopted wholeheartedly by Western peoples in their economic exploitation of the earth. The creation becomes a mere object when this view is carried to its logical conclusion. . . .
> Whether or not Christians wanted to carry their doctrine of man's dominance as far as it has been carried, the fact remains that the modern world is just now beginning to identify the Christian religion's failure to show adequate concern for the planet as a major factor in our present ecological crisis.[10]

Deloria is right in that this is the manner in which the notion of dominion over creation has been interpreted and exploited. He wrote these words two decades ago, when ecological concerns were not foremost in the agendas of most Christians—which, sadly enough, still is often the case. His interpretation of Genesis coincides with the most common interpretations among Western Christians, and on that basis he rejects Genesis as well as what he takes to be its view of our place in creation. Yet such an interpretation misreads Genesis 1. We have dominion because we are made in the image of God, whose dominion is manifested in love and in care. And our dominion does not take away from the first part of the statement, "let us *make*." We too are created, just as stones, birds, and trees are created.

> If we take that seriously, we have to image ourselves not as somehow above creation and in charge of it, but instead as one of God's created beings, related to all the rest of God's creatures: other people, the four legged, the winged, and even the trees and streams and mountains.[11]

Furthermore, if we look at Scripture this side of the Fall, we shall see that creation is not alien to God, or disconnected with redemption. Western biblical scholarship has emphasized the contrast between the religion of Israel, which sees God as the ruler of history, and the religions of the surrounding peoples, whose gods were primarily nature gods. There is much to be said for that contrast, for it is clear that in the Bible time is important, and God intervenes in history in order to bring about the divine goals. But the contrast should not be oversimplified by saying that the Judeo-Christian tradition focuses on history, and other religions focus on nature. History is not possible without nature. Because we are made out of dirt, and are tied to the earth by an umbilical cord, nature is the setting and the sustenance of history. The Lord of history can only be such by being also Lord of nature.

In the Bible, redemption is not out of nature, but in nature and through nature. The great saving act of God in the Hebrew Scriptures, the Exodus, is experienced by Israel as God's lordship over nature. In the plagues, in the opening of the sea, and in the feeding in the desert, nature is not the enemy, but rather the friend, of the people of God. Later, when the prophet speaks of the return from exile as a new and great saving act of God, he speaks of flowers blooming and fountains springing in the desert. Humans may use the Red Sea or the desert as barriers behind which to enslave people, but God and God's people see matters otherwise.

The same is true of the New Testament. When we read the stories of the "signs and wonders" of Jesus and the apostles, we tend to read them as modern Western culture has taught us: They show that Jesus and his followers have the power to suspend the order of nature, and bend it to their own ends. From this perspective, nature is a closed system, and a miracle is an event in which God does violence to that system. Over and against the "natural," stands the "supernatural," with power to interrupt the natural. In other words, the narratives regarding miracles are understood in terms of the fundamental alienation between humans and nature, and between God and nature, that we have been discussing. That, however, is not the framework within which the New Testament narratives regarding miracles are to be read. The point of such narratives is not that Jesus or the disciples do violence to nature, but rather that they are so attuned to nature, so close to its Creator, that the rest of the created order works with them, and they with it.

The same fundamental alienation from creation is operative in the notion of the "Wild West," and the manner in which most white North Americans read the history of the nation. Soon after the beginning of the European invasion of North America, the early idyllic notions of the "noble savage" gave way to the image of the "Wild West." The West was "wild" because it was untamed, and it was the task of the invaders (who usually called themselves "settlers") to tame it (or, as some would say today, to "develop" it). Creation is "fallen," and it is the task of the chosen people of God to redeem and restore it. This contrasts with the view of Chief Luther Standing Bear, which is much closer to the biblical view of creation:

> We did not think of the great open plains, the beautiful rolling hills, and winding streams with tangled growth as "wild." Only to the white men was nature a "wilderness" and only to him was the land "infested" with "wild" animals and "savage" people. To us it was tame. Earth was bountiful and we were surrounded with the blessings of the Great Mystery. Not until the hairy man from the east came and with brutal frenzy heaped injustices upon us

and the families that we loved was it "wild" for us. When the very animals of the forest began fleeing from his approach, then it was that for us the "Wild West" began.[12]

IS THERE A SOLUTION?

In summary, it would seem that we have here two contradictory and mutually exclusive perspectives. From the point of view of Native Americans, the proper starting point is creation. Although it is true that there are instances in which creation proves to be intractable and even cruel—drought, famine, and so forth—this does not mean that we must regard all creation (or all that is "wild") as essentially fallen and in need of redemption—which to many a white "developer" means subjection to "civilized" standards. From the point of view of African Americans and others such as Castuera, the experience of redemption is primary, and it is through that experience that we come to acknowledge God as creator. The two perspectives seem to be so opposed to each other that here we have reached an impasse.

Yet, the opposition between these two is not so harsh as it appears at first sight. Indeed, the reason why these two positions seem to be mutually exclusive is that we tend to look at both of them through the lens of traditional Western theology. In that theology, creation as it is described in Genesis is seen as complete, perfect within itself, with no need for change, growth, or correction. Then comes the Fall, as described in Genesis 3, and this is the basis on which any imperfection in creation is explained. Creation as it is described in Genesis 1 and 2 no longer exists. The images of alienation in Genesis 3 become the hermeneutical key for understanding the entire "history of salvation": a "paradise lost," guarded by the cherubim and by a flaming and turning sword, and an earth that now produces thorns and thistles. From that point on, and throughout all of history, we are in a grand detour—or rather, a grand return—which will find its culmination in "paradise regained." John Milton did not invent this way of reading the biblical story. By his time, it had become the standard reading in Western theology. And it remains so to this day, both among so-called liberal and among fundamentalist theologians, who may disagree on whether to take these stories literally or not, but generally agree as to their theological import.

Again, from this perspective, which has become dominant in the West, "creation" refers to an original, idyllic state of things, to the world as willed by the Creator; but between such creation and reality as it now exists stands the Fall, the reason and explanation for all evil and imperfection. This, however, is not the only possible interpretation of the biblical texts. Nor was it the only—or even the dominant—interpretation in the early church, as I have sought to show elsewhere.[13] It is also possible to look at the stories of "creation" in the early chapters of Genesis, not as "the story of creation," but as "the story of *the beginning of creation*." Indeed, it is in such terms that early Christian writers such as Irenaeus and others consistently refer to the Genesis narratives.

From this perspective, "creation" is not something that God did, which was then followed by the Fall. Creation is something God did and is still doing. History, the fact that there is movement and change within creation, is not the result of the Fall, but was always intended in God's continuing act of creation. Within that history, there have been and continue to be multiple "falls"—not only the one in Genesis 3, but also the slaying of Abel by Cain, the corruption of humankind prior to the flood, the confusion of languages at Babel, and on and on—including our own sins and the various forms of oppression humans perpetrate against one another. In other words, God's continuing act of creation is constantly engaged in a dramatic struggle with the forces of evil. Within that struggle, the "Fall" is a useful theological image, for it points to the powers of opposition, and to the manner in which they corrupt God's good creation. It is an image, however, that should be employed not to denigrate creation as it now exists, but rather to affirm its essential goodness in spite of the evil we now see at work.

From this perspective, there is a continuity between creation and redemption. Redemption is the continuing work of the Creator, as seen now in opposition to the forces of evil. It is not a last-minute solution to a world gone awry. We are not forced to choose between a Creator God and a Redeemer God, for the two are the same. As has already been said, the Logos through whom all things were made is the same One whom we now call our Redeemer. And vice versa: the Logos can be our Redeemer because "He came to what was his own" (John 1:11). As John H. Cartwright pointed out, the reason why Exodus made sense to African American slaves was that they knew themselves to be children of God, created in God's image. As he put it, in the midst of a society that often denies one's humanity, "the one place where we can go to establish our true personal value is in creation."

Thus, the first fundamental misconception we must avoid when speaking about creation is so to disjoin it from redemption—or, what is the same, from the goal of creation—that there seems to be a contradiction between the two. This would lead to sheer Marcionism, for it was Marcion who insisted on such a discontinuity between creation and redemption that the Creator could not also be the Redeemer. On the contrary, the very first act of redemption is creation itself, and every act of redemption ever since has been and will continue to be an act of creation.

CHANGE AND PERFECTION

The traditional, static notion of creation, as something fixed and finished, is closely related to a long tradition in Western thought, according to which change is an imperfection—or at least a sign of imperfection. Henry James Young was referring to that tradition when he told the Roundtable that

> the tragedy with the Platonic and Cartesian traditions in Western thought is that after being baptized into Christian theology, they tended to lead us in the direction of perceiving the static and monistic categories as intrinsically superior and the dynamic and pluralistic as intrinsically inferior.[14]

The notion that permanence is superior to change can be traced in Greek philosophy at least as far back as the Eleatic school, and it has certainly dominated most of Western philosophy. Yet this very notion, which is central to the philosophical undergirding of most traditional theology, was repeatedly questioned at the Roundtable. At its very first meeting, Jung Young Lee declared:

> My study of the *I Ching,* the earliest book on Chinese cosmology, has helped me to grasp that the concept of change is the essence of the cosmic process. . . . My theology is a reflection of my own thinking and experience of God. Since my understanding and reflection require a basic frame of reference that is change itself, the yin-yang symbol which expresses the changing process should be the foundation of my theological thinking. . . . What makes this paradigm different from other paradigms of European theologies of the past is the basic category of reality itself. The yin-yang symbol, as I said, represents a process of change. *It is change which takes the absolute category of reality. In fact reality is conceived as change rather than as being. It is not the substance that changes, but it is change that creates substance and being.*[15]

Likewise, both Young's and Castuera's approaches to creation—as well as to the rest of theology—are grounded on process philosophy, which to them is particularly valuable, among other reasons, because it places change at the very heart of being. While Castuera's use of process philosophy is more evident in work that he has done outside the Roundtable, Young made the point quite explicitly: "I find it necessary to integrate insights present in the Afro-American religious tradition and process theology. I approach the task in this manner because I am convinced that there is an affinity between the Afro-American religious heritage and process theology."[16]

In his response, Ed Wimberly challenged Young's use of process theology. Yet he did this in a manner that affirms rather than denies the importance of change. Indeed, Wimberly's objection could be interpreted as

71

arguing that process philosophy does not go far enough, for it is still too bound up in traditional intellectual categories, whereas the African American tradition, usually expressed in stories, is more dynamic.

[Young] has found process thought helpful to his own development as a theologian. However, the theological method of process thought has emerged as a form of philosophical theology that has taken the image of evolution as its major organizing image. While process thought has affinity to Afro-American religious thought, process thought itself is a method of reflection that is not employed as a method of reflection in the development of the Afro-American religious worldview. Process thought is an outgrowth of an ocular, scientific, and philosophical tradition, and the Afro-American worldview is largely the result of an oral and narrative approach to life. Relying on the narrative approach in oral tradition the Afro-American worldview developed through telling stories and listening to stories. The hermeneutical method of developing this worldview has been stories interpreting stories. Despite the differing method of hermeneutical reflection, the conclusions about creation from process thought and the Afro-American worldview are similar. However, it would be of great value to reflect on creation from an Afro-American narrative perspective and compare this reflection with process thought.[17]

There are several reasons why change is perceived as a value in many ethnic minority communities. In some cases this obviously has to do with ancient cultures and traditions that do indeed value change. Such is the case, for instance, of Dr. Lee's appeal to the yin-yang symbol and to the teachings of the *I Ching*. In most cases, there is an added socio-political dimension: People who live under conditions of oppression, and who yearn for liberation, see little hope in a static understanding of reality. In ancient Egypt, the pharaohs might have been content with their tradition of centuries, and would conceive of their task as making certain that nothing would change, that the old order would continue. The enslaved children of Israel, on the other hand, could only be helped by a God of change, by a God whose action and whose very being challenged the Egyptian status quo.

Significantly, however, philosophical notions of change are not necessarily reflected on similar notions in socio-political matters. In other words, change as an ontological value is not indissolubly connected with change as a political and social value. Indeed, several Asian Americans were quick to point out that, although change is central in the *I Ching*, it is the sort of change that leads to socio-political statism. The very notion that all is in flux, and that such change follows its own principles, may mean that one should not try to bring about change, but rather stay in one's assigned station in life. As a result, those cultures that have been most influenced by the *I Ching* are also among those that have the most rigid social hierarchies, and where women are sorely oppressed. Along these lines, Kyung-Lim Shin-Lee reminded us that, when Protestant missionaries first arrived in Korea, women heard the gospel as a message of liberation, and several were ordained. It was later, as the process for indigenization progressed, and partly through the influence of Confucianism, that the Korean church reverted to traditional patterns, prohibiting the ordination of women and in general insisting that women remain in their traditional subservient position.

Thus, the second misconception against which participants at the Roundtable cautioned was a static understanding of creation—or even a dynamic, but mechanistic one. If creation cannot change, or if all change is nothing but mechanical consequence of what went on before, there is little hope for oppressed minorities and others. Hope is precisely the expectation of change, of change that is not predetermined by existing conditions.

THE HUMAN IN THE COSMOS

Change, however, is not sufficient. Indeed, while Western philosophy and theology have tended to a static view of reality, most of the Western technocratic exploitation of the earth has been based on an unbridled thirst for change. To many a so-called developer an unspoiled wetland is an insult to human ingenuity, and must be changed. It is precisely this understanding of human "dominion" over creation that Deloria and others have so aptly criticized and that has done so much damage to the earth.

It is also necessary to clarify the place and function of humankind in the cosmos. It is clear from what has already been said that we must reject any understanding of "dominion" as having carte blanche in our dealings with the universe. It was also clear to all participants at the Roundtable that we needed to clarify our own relationship as humans to the rest of the created universe.

At the very first session of the Roundtable, even before our topics for discussion were outlined and clarified, Jung Young Lee said:

> I have come to notice that cosmology is more important than anthropology in the Chinese and Korean ways of thinking. The reason is that human beings are considered to be part of the cosmos. Understanding the cosmos, therefore, implies the understanding of human nature as well. Moreover, the cosmos and the ultimate reality are inseparably related and mutually inclusive in Eastern traditions.[18]

Henry Young argues that, although there are significant differences among various African religious traditions, they all affirm what he calls "the organic world view." This rejects both the Western tendency to build a gulf between the religious and the secular, and Western individualism.

Referring to Descartes, who began with his famous *cogito ergo sum,* and arrived at the dualistic notion of a spiritual and a material reality, Young suggests that a better starting point would be *cognatus ergo sum*—I am related, therefore I am. (A view that is also reflected in the traditional phrase of the Native American sweatlodge, "all my relatives," which reminds all participants that each one of us is related to the entire world.) This is one of the reasons why Young finds process theology of value to his theological undertaking.

> Process theology is compatible with the African world view in its recognition that reality is socialized rather than individualized. By this is meant that everything in the world is inextricably bound together into a web of interdependence. Each aspect of existence is interrelated with every other aspect. Nothing exists in separation and isolation. This makes relationality characteristic to all dimensions of existence. No longer can we think of reality as autonomous, independent and separate. Each aspect of reality is socialized in the sense that whatever affects any reality directly automatically affects the whole of reality indirectly. To be socialized means to be interwoven both internally and externally. Because social relatedness is characteristic of the nature of reality, it has profound implication for understanding God's continued creativity in the world.[19]

Obviously, the use of societal imagery must not be understood in anthropocentric terms, as referring only to interpersonal relationships. On the contrary, what Young means is that all of reality is a single society, so that all things are interrelated, and that human beings are one element in the web of that vast society of interdependence.

Ignacio Castuera argued along similar lines, hoping for a doctrine of creation that would build on that attitude of ethnic minorities which "North European peoples have generally described as a laid back attitude toward nature, but which reflects a desire to move with the natural rhythm and direction instead of seeing nature as something to struggle against and overcome."[20] On this basis, he insists that "human rights" must be extended to "nature rights," for just as humans have no right to exploit one another and to deprive one another of their dignity, so do we have no right to exploit nature and to deprive it of its own worth and beauty.

A similar note was sounded, if anything more insistently and passionately, by Native Americans. As Sam Wynn put it, "The Native American experienced and understood creation through nature, respect for nature, and a close feeling of kinship with the animals and all living things, human or not."[21] To this, Sue Ellen Herne, a Mohawk, agreed: "The actual event of creation is interpreted in order for us to begin to understand our place within creation."[22]

Native Americans who look to their traditional spiritual roots often find deepening ties not only to the earth in general, but to specific places of significance. Sacred sites are integral to the practice of many Native American religions. This tie between the Creator, the earth, and the people has often been desecrated by those who fail to understand it.

> As for the Indians, there were thousands of them in the sacred places of Paha-Sapa, the Black Hills. It was summer, the time for communing with the Great Spirit, for beseeching his pity and seeking visions. Members of all the tribes were there at the center of the world, singly or in small bands, engaged in these religious ceremonies. They watched the dust streamers of two thousand soldiers and their horses and wagons, and hated them for their desecration of Paha-Sapa, from where the hoop of the world bent to the four directions. But no war parties were formed, and the Indians kept away from the noisy, dusty column.[23]

These sacred sites retain their importance for traditional North Americans. Parallels in Scripture can be found in many passages where a specific place is significant—from the place where Jacob lay his head in Genesis 28:10-22, to the city of Jerusalem.

And from an Asian American perspective come the following words:

> Asian people are conditioned by the cycle of rural life and are therefore endowed with a sure confidence that the forces of nature/seasons are powerfully and quietly at work. Westerners often confuse this as a lack of assertiveness or refusal to take control. This patient waiting is a part of Asian-American spirituality by which suffering and pain is not only endured but a source of hope.[24]

Thus, a third fundamental misconception when speaking about creation is to speak as if we somehow stood outside creation. We are creatures, and as such are part of creation. This is not a limitation but is part of our very essence. We cannot stand outside creation, as independent beings, or as demigods. The importance of this is not only theoretical or doctrinal, but has much to do with the manner in which we deal with the rest of creation. Beings that are not part of creation, but that in a sense are mere sojourners in it, could afford to mistreat creation; but we are not such beings, and therefore, whatever we do to creation we do to ourselves, for we are inexorably part of it—as Young would say, we are bound with it in a "web of interdependence."

Such a "web of interdependence" belies any hierarchical understanding of creation. This must be pointed out, since hierarchical views of creation have appeared repeatedly throughout the history of Christian thought. At the high point of the Middle Ages, mostly through the influence of Pseudo-Dionysius, the entire universe, and even the Godhead, was conceived as a series of hierarchies. The Trinity itself was seen as a hierarchy, whose tripartite order was then reflected in all of creation. There was a hierarchy of angelic beings, and a hierarchy of demons. The church, like all the rest of creation, was by nature hierarchical. The closer any being was to God, the higher its place in the hierarchical structure of the universe. Since God is above all powerful and spiritual, these two were also the characteristics of the higher order of being. Spiritual beings or "intellects" were considered superior to bodies, and the powerful were thought to reflect God's power.

Although most people today no longer believe in neat classifications of angelic and demonic hierarchies, the essence of the hierarchical world view still remains. Some beings are more important than others. The "spiritual" is more important than the "material." The "leaders" are more important than the "followers." The powerful resemble God more closely than the powerless. Woman was created after man, and therefore must be subject to him. All these opinions, which one hears repeatedly, stand at the root of racism, classism, sexism, and ageism. If, on the other hand, creation, rather than a hierarchy, is a "web of interdependence," such hierarchical and oppressive perspectives and practices must be challenged.

CREATION, STEWARDSHIP, WORK, AND LEISURE

The image theology uses most commonly today to refer to the manner in which we are to relate to creation is "stewardship." Although this is a term that is usually related to the task of raising funds for the church, Castuera is quite right when he declares that this term "needs to be used in our circles not only during our financial campaigns, but as a foundational idea for the care of the earth in its most comprehensive way." [25] And Young, speaking from the African American perspective, agrees: "In African Religion humanity is perceived as 'the steward' of God's creation." [26] This is certainly a biblical image, one that appears frequently in the parables of Jesus.

There are, however, several clarifications that must be made regarding stewardship. At this point, one could begin with the traditional stewardship sermon, at least as it used to be when I was growing up. The argument of those sermons, in a nutshell, is: All that you have belongs to God, and God has given it to you so that you may manage it. I myself have preached that sermon countless times, with countless different biblical texts as a pretext.

However, when one stops to think about it, there clearly is a preceding question that must be asked: Can we really claim that all we have has been given to us by God? Is that true in any and all circumstances? Suppose, for instance, that I hold up a bank. Can I claim that, since I have this money, God has given it to me so that I may manage it? Clearly not. I simply took it. In such circumstances, to say that all we have has been given to us by God is to blame God for our greed and for our illegal and unjust having.

Thus, although it is true that whatever we *legitimately* have is given to us so that we may manage it on God's behalf, we must take care not to say that anything we have, no matter how acquired, has been given to us by God—a particularly important point when it comes to the ownership of land, where most having and holding is the result of invasion and conquest, as Native Americans correctly remind us.

Or suppose that, for whatever reasons, I have ample money, and food, and shelter, and more clothing than I can possibly wear, while around me there are others who have no money, and no food, and no shelter, and nothing to wear. If I say that whatever I have, God has given me so that I may manage it, am I not implying that whatever those others do not have, God has not given them, and that therefore their poverty, hunger, homelessness, and nakedness are the will of God? We must take care, lest in saying, for instance, that all food belongs to God and is therefore given by God, we blame God for hunger.

The problem here is that we often forget who a steward was at the time when Jesus spoke his parables. A steward was normally a slave. The steward himself belonged to the master, and it was only as a servant of the ultimate owner that he held any authority. A mismanaged stewardship is no longer such.

If, on that basis, we look again at the assertion that all we have is given to us by God, in order to administer it for the divine purposes, we begin to see the radical implications of such an affirmation. It clearly implies that any having that is not from God, or that does not serve God's purposes, is not legitimate having. From this perspective, the only legitimate test for whether I truly own a farm or not, is not whether I have a deed, or can prove in a court of law that I paid for it, but whether or not both my having it and my use of it are consistent with God's purposes. Obviously, we do not know exactly what God's purposes are, and there is ample room here for opinion and debate. But there are certain things that we definitely know are *not* God's purposes: oppression, exploitation, injustice, death. Thus, any owning or having which is used in oppressive or exploitative ways may be legal; but it certainly is not legitimate in God's eyes. When land is taken from those who used it to grow food, or to fish and hunt, in order to exploit it "more efficiently," such ownership, even though sanctioned by law, is not legitimate; and we cannot begin a stewardship sermon in such a setting by saying, "All that you have God gave you so that you might administer it in God's name." Or, when ownership of land is used to exploit and poison migrant workers, a true understanding of stewardship should lead us to question, not only the labor practices of the owners, but even their right to own the land. This is a doctrine not often preached in our churches, but which was part of the standard teaching of the early church.[27]

Then, there is another important element in the notion of stewardship that we often forget. In many of the parables quoted in connection with stewardship, there is a master, an owner; but in them also the master is absent. Indeed, the theme of the absence of the master runs through those parables. Matthew 25: "For it is as if a man, going on a journey, summoned his slaves and entrusted his property to them; to one he gave five talents, to another two, to another one, to each according to his ability. Then he went away." Matthew 25 again: "Ten bridesmaids took their lamps and went to meet the bridegroom. . . . [But] the bridegroom was delayed." Matthew 24: "But if that wicked slave says to himself, 'my master is delayed,' . . . the master of that slave will come . . ." Matthew 21: "There was a landowner who planted a vineyard, put a fence around it, dug a wine press in it, and built a watchtower. Then he leased it to tenants and went to another country."

We often speak of the presence of God, and rightly so. But this other theme or metaphor of absence is also present in the Bible. Even apart from sin, God gives the human creature space, freedom to exercise its responsibility. In the story in the garden, after creating humankind, and giving them dominion over the rest of creation, God lets them exercise that dominion, even though it also implies the possibility of sin. And this absence, just as much as the divine presence, is a sign of love, just as a parent out of love finds it necessary to step back and let a child try his or her wings, even at the risk of pain and failure. A parent who is always present, guarding a child from every risk and every hurt, is not a very good parent. Even apart from sin, God's absence, the space that God gives us to grow, to be responsible, to try our wings, is a sign of God's love.

Once one takes sin into consideration, however, the divine absence has an added dimension. This is indeed God's world. But it is God's rebellious world. This world, made by God, is also godless. In this godless world of God, the image that appears so frequently in the parables, of the absence of the master, is both a realistic description of our present situation and a call to responsibility. While the master is away, the steward must run things according to the will of the absent master. We still do not see the glory of the reign of God. We still do not see justice being done for the weak sheep that have been pushed aside by the strong (Ezek. 34:31). We still do not see the peace and security and justice that is God's will. And yet, we know that this is God's world. The master who is away is still the legitimate and sole owner, and as long as the absence lasts we have no option but to do the master's will. (At this point, it may be well to point out the contrast between what is expected of us in these parables, where the legitimate master is absent, and the attitude expressed in a traditional song toward an illegitimate master: "Jimmy crack corn and I don't care; the master's gone away.")

The absence of the legitimate master provides an opportunity for true stewards to exercise their freedom and their obedience. Yet it also provides opportunity for the "wicked steward"—which is also a biblical image. The wicked steward is the one who takes the opportunity of the master's absence to become a false master, to oppress and to exploit.

It is because of wicked stewards that various groups in society are oppressed, and the earth is exploited to such a point that survival itself is at risk. The "absence" of God—the space provided by God for human freedom and legitimate stewardship—is used by wicked stewards to create a godless world.

Ethnic minorities, women, and other oppressed groups do not need to be told that this is a godless world. The suffering of generations is ample proof of that. A Native American who pays an outrageous rent for a tiny apartment built on land where her ancestors lived, and who has no money to pay for medical attention for her children, does not have to be told that there is suffering in the world. A Mexican American working with his family picking grapes, and knowing that jointly with the grapes they are collecting poison which will shorten their lives, does not need to be told that there is suffering in the world. An African American trying to rear her children in a ghetto where many young people see dealing in drugs as the only possible way out, and where police no longer even attempt to keep a modicum of order, does not have to be told that there is suffering in the world.

Out of such experiences, the godlessness of God's world, or the question of theodicy, was also posed in several of our discussions. As Henry Young stated, "Any discussion of creation must involve responding to the age old dilemma of theodicy, namely, why do the righteous suffer? The continued suffering of Afro-Americans and other oppressed minority groups tends to heighten our awareness of the problem."[28]

Significantly, however, as our discussion proceeded we found ourselves reversing the manner in which the matter of theodicy has usually been discussed. What we were dealing with was not so much the question of how to reconcile God's goodness with evil: How can there be a good God, when there is so much evil in the world? Rather, what we found to be a common attitude among our people is precisely the reverse: Because there is so much evil in the world, there must be a good God. This in no way diminishes the pain and the tragedy of evil. Nor does it simply dissolve evil into joy. On the contrary, what it means is that the experience of evil among oppressed peoples is such and so constant, that what is surprising is not evil, but survival. This may have something to do with what Stephen Kim mentioned in his paper, that the apparent injustice in the parable of the laborers surprises only those who expect life to be fair, who have grown up in settings where logic seems to apply, and where laws work in their favor.[29] People who are treated with respect when they go to a police station to complain about something, and whose job application is taken seriously on the basis of their qualifications, expect life to be fair. People who are often considered guilty before being allowed even to state their case, whose qualifications for a job are doubted because of their race or gender, and who bear the marks of an ages-long struggle for survival against all odds, do not expect life to be fair. Those who are used to an order—or disorder—where injustice reigns, and where the stronger prevail, are surprised, not by the existence of evil, but by the fact that it does not conquer all; surprised, not by evil, but by good. For them, evil, rather than questioning the existence or the goodness of God, confirms it.

It is within this world, where evil is a common experience, but which is still God's good creation, that we are called to be stewards. Stewardship is an image whose value lies precisely in that it retains the tension between our owning and not owning, and between this being God's world and this being also a world from which God is absent.

Oddly enough, to affirm too glibly that everything belongs to God can be an easy way of avoiding the will of God. The world is God's, yes; but it is also ours to manage as stewards. It is we, humankind, who have been given responsibility for it, and it is we who have messed it up, both for humankind and for the rest of creation. We are not in the world as mere spectators, nor as absolute owners, but as stewards of a world of which we are also a part, until the day when we must render account to its ultimate owner.

Stewardship implies that, much popular theology notwithstanding, work is *not* the result of the Fall. In the Genesis story, even before the Fall, the human creature is given a garden to till. Tilling is not the result of the Fall. Tilling is part of God's purpose in creation. The reason for this, as was pointed out earlier, is that God's creative activity and purposes are not exhausted by a primal act of bringing things into being. What Genesis 1 and 2 depict is "the beginning of creation." Creation continues throughout all of history. In this creation, the human creature plays a significant role as God's steward. The garden is given as a place for work. It is humanity's responsibility to employ God's gift of a good earth, good plants, and so on, to make the garden become what it ought to be. In the Genesis story, work is not a curse; what is a curse is fruitless, meaningless toil, as when the tilled soil produces thorns and thistles. This is important. The doctrine of creation applies, not only to the natural, but also to that which humanity has created as God's stewards. The doctrine of creation does not necessarily lead to an opposition between the "natural" and the "artificial," as if all that is made by human effort were of necessity evil or inferior. The human creature is intended by God to work, to till, to "make a living" in the midst of creation, to be an "artificer." Therefore the result of the human "arts," the "artificial," is as much part of God's creation as nature itself. Clearly, because humans are who we are, our "artifacts" are tainted by sin. We are intended to "*cult*ivate," and therefore, even though our "*cult*ures" are certainly not pure or perfect, the fact that there is culture and cultivation is part of God's good creation.

Stewardship also implies that this is a world from which God is in a sense absent. God does not control the world in such a way as to leave us nothing to do, but rather leaves us space to be responsible. The divine absence provides the space for stewardship—as Scripture says, "The Master went to a far away country." It also provides the opportunity for sin, so that it is possible to speak of creation as God's godless world.

The godlessness of the world, the very absence of God, also provides the opportunity for our meeting God. We often think that the best place to meet God is where God's will is being done—among the "best" people of society and in the most religious places. Yet, that is not what Matthew 25 says. According to that text, we shall meet the Lord among the hungry, the naked, and the jailed—precisely in those places where God's will is not being done. The significance of this point for ethnic minorities should be obvious, since it is precisely among the hungry, the naked, and those in jail that our people are not a minority!

THE SEVENTH DAY OF CREATION

Lest we take ourselves and our work too seriously, however, Castuera reminded us that the crown of creation is not humankind, but God's rest. In the biblical account, there are not six, but seven days of creation; and the culmination of it all is the day God rested. He rightly relates the seventh day with what has been said regarding "dominion":

> Many Old Testament scholars and theologians are persuaded that it is necessary to remind ourselves that the creation myth states that God created the world in seven, rather than in six, days. This is important because the crowning event in the creation story is the day of rest instead of the creation of humanity.
>
> This is a most important insight because much of the misreading of the meaning of the word "dominion" stems from the false perception that we humans are at the top of the heap, so to speak. God's sovereignty is at the top of the creation event. God's rest, or the creation of the Sabbath, is the capstone of God's action as creator.[30]

This leads Castuera to insist on the need to devise and advocate for a rhythm of creative work and leisure. Against the evil of unemployment, which so affects our minority communities, "We must insist that society make adequate provision for jobs and wages which permit the exercise of the creative forces within our people."[31] (These words reminded me of a sermon I heard in Colombia, South America, in which a Pentecostal preacher, on a series of sermons on the Ten Commandments, came to the subject of the Sabbath. His point was not, as is common among those who have adequate employment, that we must rest on the seventh day, but rather that those structures and individuals which prevent us from having creative employment the rest of the week are preventing us from keeping the law of God!) On the other hand, against a society in which activism has reached such a point that even leisure must be filled with activity, Castuera argued for a recovery of the true sense of rest and play:

> The playful side of our humanity must be emphasized and protected if we are to be truly influenced by the doctrine of creation. Capitalism and Marxism have overemphasized the working side of humanity. *Homo faber*, the human as worker, has been the dominant image in these systems at the expense of *homo ludens*, the human as playful.[32]

By this, Castuera does not mean that we must have more leisure activities. His concern is that, precisely because we have emphasized activity and doing as essential to the *homo faber*, even our understanding of leisure is now corrupted by an activism, an anxiety of doing, which destroys the proper rhythm between creation and rest. We must be doing, producing, purposeful, not only in our work, but also in our leisure, which in consequence is no longer a true sabbath rest.

God rested. The final word about creation is not one of action and productivity, but of rest. We are called to work, to change the world, to join God in the work of creation. But the Creator God, who calls us to creative activity, also calls us to rest. It may be in our capacity for rest, as well as in our capacity for work, that our faith and trust in the Creator God is proved.

CHAPTER FIVE

VISIONS OF SALVATION

SALVATION, STRUGGLE, AND SURVIVAL

Much Christian preaching seeks to answer the question of the jailer in Philippi, "What must I do to be saved?" Yet, we seldom stop to ask the first question, What do we mean by salvation? For that reason, the theme for the 1989 session of the Roundtable of Ethnic Theologians was "Salvation, Struggle, Survival." As that theme was announced, the Planning Team declared: "We have chosen these terms out of the intuition that we will understand the meaning of salvation much better as we relate it to the struggle for survival among our people. This means both the individual daily survival and our survival as a people or a culture."

That "intuition" proved to be supported by the presenters. Japanese American Lloyd K. Wake expressed the connection in the following terms:

> For Asian-Americans, salvation goes beyond a theological doctrine, or a metaphysical concept. It relates to rice and tea issues of survival—identity, self-worth, personal and community dignity, self-determination, justice and physical existence in a physical place. It is the well-being not only of the soul and spirit, but of the body. Salvation is materialistic, incarnational, and grounded in history.[1]

In various ways, all the other presenters reflected similar sentiments. Puerto Rican Ediberto López said that "our way of walking in faith, of walking in the Spirit, will be through a political, cultural, ideological and personal life that rejects any instance of oppression and tries to build a humane society for Latinos."[2] And in their respective papers, both Tweedy Evelene Sombrero (Navajo) and Cain H. Felder (African American) add to this the ecological dimension of salvation having to do, not only with ourselves or with humankind, but with the entire world. Recalling her pain when she saw strip mining for the first time, Sombrero quoted the words of an older member of her tribe: "We are digging into the earth because we don't care for each other anymore. We need to care for each other, for everybody, or the earth will die, and so will we." As she then expressed it in her presentation,

> Are we willing to come together as humans to start this healing process, for this is our salvation? Because of my interrelatedness with the earth, then, I am related to all creation in the world—this means the four-legged, two-legged, winged creation and all the created order.[3]

In the conversation that followed, Felder affirmed that the question of survival is prior to the question of salvation, for we are now pressed by the urgent question of cosmic survival, which goes far beyond the issue of private, personal survival. As a series of concentric circles, he expanded the issue from personal survival to the survival of ethnic groups and cultures, to the survival of the human race, and finally to the survival of the planet.

As the conversation proceeded, it was clear to all of us that it is necessary to widen the understanding of salvation as it has been taught and preached by much of traditional Christian theology.

The first and most obvious point at which the common understanding of salvation needs to be widened is in its scope. In most traditional Christianity, when one speaks of "salvation" what one really means is "spiritual salvation." This includes both the assurance that one will live beyond death in the presence of God, and a sense of inner peace and well-being that is derived from that assurance.

Although this dimension of salvation must not be denied, all the presenters at the Roundtable insisted that there is another, equally important dimension, which must not be forgotten. This is why, in the statement just quoted, Wake calls for an understanding of salvation that is "materialistic, incarnational, and grounded in history."

The joining of the terms "survival" and "salvation" facilitated our discussion on this point. For many of us, one of the essential elements of salvation is survival. This does not mean that one must first of all save one's own skin in order to be saved. Such a view would certainly be anti-biblical, and goes against all that Jesus said about having to lose one's life in order to save it. What the connection with survival does mean is that in the biblical view salvation is closely related to survival, and is often manifested as survival—though often of a group, of the people of God, rather than of an individual.

In the Hebrew Scriptures, God's great saving act is the opening of the

Red Sea so that the people may flee from the yoke of Egypt. God saves Israel out of Egypt by giving them space for survival. Likewise, when the people are oppressed, God lifts up for them a "savior" whose task is to free them from their oppression: "Therefore the Lord gave Israel a savior, so that they escaped from the hand of the Arameans; and the people of Israel lived in their homes as formerly" (II Kings 13:5). And, "When they cry to the Lord because of oppressors, he will send them a savior, and will defend and deliver them" (Isa. 19:20). It is clear that in all these cases, and in many others that could be cited, "salvation" means survival with dignity as a free people.

The same is true in the New Testament. The same Greek word is sometimes translated into English as "save," and sometimes as "heal." Clearly, there are different connotations in various passages where that word is used, and that is the reason for the different words in translation. But by making such a sharp distinction the translators are deciding that there are two almost unrelated realities, one having to do with the body and one with the soul. It would be grammatically correct, for instance, to translate the words of the woman suffering from hemorrhages as "If I only touch his cloak, I will be saved" (Matt. 9:21). And Jairus may have pleaded: "My little daughter is at the point of death. Come and lay your hands on her, so that she may be saved, and live" (Mark 5:23). On the other hand, the oft-quoted words of Peter at Pentecost could also be translated as "Everyone who calls on the name of the Lord shall be healed" (Acts 2:21). And the famous words of Paul to the Corinthians could be read as "God decided, through the foolishness of our proclamation, to heal those who believe" (I Cor. 1:21).

Again, this does not mean that wherever our English Bibles say "save" we should read "heal," and vice versa. What it does mean is that salvation is much closer to healing, and healing closer to salvation, than we usually imagine. Although there may be a difference in emphasis that legitimates the difference in translations between "to heal" and "to save," that difference must not be exaggerated to such a point that it becomes a contrast between the two.

Yet, much traditional theology has fallen precisely into such an exaggeration. When some traditional theologians write about "soteriology"— the doctrine of salvation—what they deal with is how one's soul is saved from eternal damnation, how one's sins may be forgiven, what "eternal life" means, and so forth. They do not deal with the relationship between all of these things and physical disease, or political and economic oppression.

Quite clearly, the scope of salvation is not exhausted by healing or by liberation, although it certainly includes them. When the early Christian martyrs gave up their lives rather than betray their Lord, they were not "saved" in the sense of being delivered from the lions or liberated from the power of the Empire to do them physical harm; but they certainly attained salvation. Salvation involves victory and survival against all oppressive enemies of humankind—and that includes death itself. Indeed, there are times and situations when the only salvation attainable is that which consists in victory beyond death. Such was the case of the early martyrs. Such was the case of many a slave laboring on a plantation. Such is still the case of many an oppressed person, both in this country and beyond. Furthermore, it is clear that ultimate and complete salvation can be attained only when death itself is conquered, and therefore it is not attainable in this life. Yet, it is also true that full salvation begins in this life, and takes the form of healing, survival, and liberation.

THE EARLY SETTING

In this regard, the Christian doctrine of salvation has had an interesting history. Christianity came into the Mediterranean world at a time when many of the old religions were losing their grip on the people. Those old religions had evolved at a much earlier time, when religious and civic allegiance went hand in hand with each other. The gods of an ancient Athenian or Roman were those of Athens or Rome. One had to make no decision as to which gods to believe in, just as one had made no decision as to where to be born. One might have a preference for some of the many gods available, depending on one's interests, occupation, and so on. But the choice of gods was not a matter of urgent or paramount importance.

Then came the growth of empires, and with it the confusion of the gods. When Alexander conquered Egypt, he was made a god by the Egyptians. This was a sign of things to come. By the time Christianity appeared on the scene, all the Mediterranean basin was under Roman rule. Although people could still hold citizenship in various cities, in fact the urban population throughout the Empire was highly mobile. Romans, Carthaginians, Alexandrians, and Athenians all rubbed elbows in a city such as Corinth. For them the old gods, whose main interest and function was to protect the ancient city-state, no longer served. It is true that some people continued serving them, and that there was an attempt to make them more cosmopolitan by establishing equations between various gods, so that Neptune and Poseidon were said to be the same, and so were Venus and Aphrodite. Yet in a world in which people no longer knew their place by virtue of birth, they also no longer knew their religion on the basis of their citizenship.

There is a great contrast between the world of Plato, in the fourth century B.C., and the world of Marcus Aurelius, in the second century A.D. Although Plato's dialogues would eventually have vast influence throughout the world, his own vision of the world was rather limited. His horizon was practically that of Athens and of the city-state. When he wrote about an ideal Republic, he was not thinking, as we are today, of an area of several thousand square miles and millions of citizens. He was thinking of a city very similar in size to Athens. In contrast, when Marcus Aurelius wrote his *Soliloquies,* in the second century A.D., he was at the very center of a vast empire in which many cultures, languages, and traditions mingled. He himself, though living in Rome as head of the Roman Empire, wrote in Greek, and his universe was much wider than Plato's. As he said, "As an Antonine, my land is Rome; as a human, it is the world. All that is good for these two lands is also good for me." The contrast between Plato and Marcus Aurelius—and between their respective times—goes far beyond the size of their world. It is significant that Plato wrote "dialogues" for publication and for the uplifting of the best among the citizens of Athens, whereas Marcus Aurelius wrote "soliloquies" for his own use, without intending that they ever be read by another. Plato, though the disciple of a man condemned to death for corrupting the youth of the city, felt quite at home in Athens. Marcus Aurelius, even though ruler of the world, was no longer at home in that world, which was too big even for him, and thus in his moments of greatest authenticity tended to withdraw within himself, and to devote himself to soliloquies.

The world into which Christianity first made its appearance has been described as "cosmopolitan." That is a significant word, which for Plato would have implied a contradiction, for it seems to equate the vast, ungraspable "cosmos" with the more limited unit of the "polis." To be a "citizen" of the "cosmos," as Marcus Aurelius claimed, meant that the city had expanded to such a point as to embrace the entire cosmos. This was certainly a hyperbole, but one that adequately depicted the "cosmopolitan" world in which Christianity made its appearance.

In such a cosmopolitan world, the meaning of life is also in question. The good of the state, for which many an ancient Athenian or Roman had lived in earlier times, was no longer a viable goal for people lost in the vastness of the Roman Empire.

It was in response to that situation, and to the yearnings produced by it, that many a religion arose whose attraction was in offering salvation out of this confused world. The mysteries, which had existed from ancient times as ways of relating to the myths of origins and to the seasonal death and resurrection of nature, now became means whereby individuals could attain "salvation"—meaning continued life after death. Classical Greek philosophy, which had always been preoccupied with the meaning of life and human destiny, now evolved in such a way as to become in itself a way of salvation.

Of all these religions offering "salvation," probably the most alluring was Gnosticism, a vast religious movement of obscure and mixed origins which flourished during the first centuries of the Christian era. There is much debate as to the origins of Gnosticism, and just as much as to its exact nature. This is not the place to enter such a debate. However, it is clear that Gnosticism was above all a religion—or a conglomerate of religions—of salvation. The Gnostics saw the world as an alien place in which human spirits are entrapped. All the world, even one's own body, is part of that structure of bondage. Above the physical earth, there are several spheres—a common element in the astronomy of the times—and each of these spheres is an obstacle between us and "salvation," or, as many called it, the "fullness." The goal of life is to escape from this prison, making one's way through the spheres of entrapment, and thus eventually to reach the purely spiritual, which is our true abode.

Orthodox Christianity fought a hard battle against Gnosticism and other similar doctrines—particularly against those who sought to combine Christianity with their Gnostic views. To many Christian leaders, Gnosticism seemed to deny the basic tenets of the Christian faith. By declaring the world an evil place, and ascribing evil to matter and good to spirit, the Gnostics contradicted the Christian doctrine of creation, which affirmed the essential goodness of all creation—material as well as spiritual. Some of the Gnostics also denied the incarnation of God in Jesus Christ, for the true, spiritual God cannot be incarnate in a body of flesh and bones. The struggle was long, and at times the outcome seemed to be in doubt. It was as a result of that struggle that a list of New Testament books evolved, as well as several creeds and other means to distinguish the orthodox from the heretical.

Eventually, Gnosticism was defeated. The Scriptures the Gnostics rejected—including in many cases all the Old Testament—were reaffirmed by the church. The speculations of the Gnostics about the "eons" and the origin of this material world were rejected. The church reaffirmed the doctrines of creation and of incarnation. The names of the great Gnostic teachers were almost forgotten.

This was achieved through two means. The first and most obvious was the tightening of the organization of the church.[4] Bishops and elders were given greater authority, and their connection with the apostles was emphasized. There was a movement to fix the liturgy, so that extraneous elements could not be surreptitiously introduced. Creeds were formulated to serve as touchstones to prove that one affirmed the essential tenets of orthodox Christianity which the heretics denied. The formation of the canon of Scripture, to which I referred in the second chapter, was part of this process. Through all these measures, the church assured itself that those who openly taught Gnostic doctrine would be excluded from its ranks.

This is not to say that the entire process whereby the church became organized into a vast connectional network throughout the Empire and even beyond was a reaction to Gnosticism, or that it was a negative development. On the contrary, it was in part a very positive and necessary response to the very situation which made Gnosticism so attractive. In the midst of a world so vast, so fluctuating, and so confused that people no longer had a sense of place or worth, the church became a way of belonging. Being "saved" thus meant not only being assured of a life beyond death, but also being assured of a place and a worth in this life. In this state of affairs, it is not difficult to imagine the impact of Paul's words, "So let no one boast about human leaders. For all things are yours, whether Paul or Apollos or Cephas or the world or life or death or the present or the future—all belong to you, and you belong to Christ, and Christ belongs to God" (I Cor. 3:21-23). To this we shall return in the next chapter, when discussing the doctrine of the church.

The second means whereby the orthodox church managed to defeat Gnosticism was not nearly so obvious: To a large degree, the church coopted the Gnostic view of salvation, and made it its own. This was Gnosticism's greatest attraction, for it seemed to respond to the deepest yearnings of people caught and lost in the vast cosmopolitan turbulence of late antiquity.[5] Obviously, orthodox Christianity never officially accepted the most flagrantly heterodox elements in the Gnostic understanding of salvation. Theologians rejected, for instance, the notion that we are fallen spirits of celestial origin, trapped in this world by error and ignorance. Yet they accepted and coopted the basic structure of Gnostic soteriology.

The result was an understanding of salvation that, without falling into the speculations of traditional Gnosticism, was—and is—essentially Gnostic. According to this understanding, salvation is a "spiritual" matter, having little or nothing to do with the material world. What is to be saved—in many cases, at least in the most popular versions, the only element of human life that can be saved—is the soul. The "gospel" then is good news, not about the entirety of life, but about the eternal destiny of one's soul. Any relationship it might have with issues such as hunger, oppression, and social justice is merely tangential and secondary, for these are no longer issues of "salvation." It is this semi-Gnostic view of salvation as having nothing to do with the material that has led to the sharp distinction in our translations between "salvation" and "healing" already discussed, and which has no grammatical or lexicographical basis in the original text.

Such a view of salvation, however, is incompatible with the doctrine of creation—which the church reaffirmed precisely in its struggle against Gnosticism. If salvation is at least in part a restoration of God's creation, and all of God's creation is good, salvation must have something to do with the entirety of that creation, and not only with the spiritual. When Genesis says about creation that "it was good," it is not speaking of spiritual creation as opposed to the material, but of all of creation. Therefore, a purely "spiritual" salvation, with no "material" dimensions, is not biblical.

This semi-Gnostic view of salvation has contributed to a disparagement of the "Old" Testament by many Christians—an attitude that is parallel to that of many Gnostics and of Marcion. Indeed, if the central message of the Bible is that our souls can be saved and live eternally, then the Hebrew Scriptures are at best prolegomena to the real message, and at worst a misunderstanding of the message itself. In the "books of Moses," God's "salvation" is the deliverance from Egypt. In Judges, "salvation" is a successful uprising against oppressors. In Isaiah and several of the prophets, it is freedom and return from exile. In the Psalms, it is the destruction of one's enemies. If all of this has nothing to do with "real salvation," then it is difficult to see why these books are considered sacred and inspired Scripture.

This view of salvation has also distorted our understanding of God, at least in popular religiosity. According to a commonly held view, and one heard often in "evangelistic" preaching, the great enemy from whom we have to be saved is not Satan, but God! It is God who is so angry at us—indeed, at all of humankind—that if not appeased will send us all to eternal damnation. The "justice" of God is such that it demands blood—if not our own, then that of Jesus. The result in much popular piety is that God the Father becomes the judge, the wrathful one, even the enemy, whereas "sweet Jesus" becomes the forgiving friend, the loving one.[6] Needless to say, this goes against all that the church has ever officially taught regarding the doctrine of the Trinity. It also goes against the biblical witness, where there is no such dichotomy in the Godhead. Actually, it comes extremely close to the teachings of Marcion and many of the Gnostics, for whom the creator—or creators—was different and radically opposed to the Redeemer. The result is a strange sort of "good news" message whose first item of news is that we are all sinners, that God is enraged at us, and that we are going directly to hell. It is the "good news" that all of what our ancestors did is from Satan and must be abandoned—as was the case for Marvin Abrams, who was taught not to approach the longhouse, lest God become angry with him, and condemn him to hell. One wonders, how is this "good" news?

THE EARLY CENTURIES, AND OURS

There is more here than meets the eye, for the manner in which one understands the saving work of Jesus will greatly determine the manner in which one understands one's own responsibility as a Christian today. If Christ became the Savior by becoming the victim, then there is no better way to follow him than by being a victim. This may be a necessary word for those whose position in society is such that they tend to be the victimizers rather than the victims. But it is not a helpful or a saving word for those whom society constantly and repeatedly victimizes. If there is something positive and redemptive about being a victim, then the poor should be content with their situation, for in that situation, and especially in accepting it as a lamb led to the slaughter, they are most like Jesus. As Lloyd Wake put it, "The concept that His [Jesus'] death, regardless of how heroic, could 'pay for' humankind's sins . . . engenders passivity." [7]

We may be used to reading the gospel in such terms; yet that is not what the gospels tell us of Jesus. On the contrary, they present him as a strong person who repeatedly rebuked the prestigious in his society, who broke all respectable social conventions by eating with sinners, who called Herod a "fox," who "set his face" to go to Jerusalem, in order there to challenge the structures of power. As he put it, his life was not taken from him; rather, he lay it down in order to take it up again. Or, as the epistle to the Ephesians expresses it, he descended, not because he was broken and passive, but rather so that on ascending he could make "captivity itself a captive," and give "gifts to his people" (Eph. 4:8). His death is redemptive, not because it is the death of a poor devil who could not do otherwise, and meekly submitted to it, but rather because it is the powerful death of One who could indeed do otherwise, but who out of solidarity with suffering humankind underwent death in order to wrest victory for his people from the very depths of Hades.

Significantly, here too the Gnostic understanding of salvation has played a role in later Christian views. The Gnostics believed that, in order to be saved, what one needed was a special sort of knowledge. In some Gnostic systems, what this meant specifically was that one had to know a secret password to be let through each of the encircling spheres, as one progressed in the ascent to the "fullness." Oddly enough, much of today's Christian preaching seems to employ the name of Jesus in a similar way, as a sort of talisman whose possession ensures one's safe passage, if not through the encircling spheres, at least through the pearly gates. "All you need to do is believe in Jesus," we are told, "and you will be saved."

The words of such preaching may be true, but the message conveyed often is not. What is usually understood by these words is that the same legalistic, cruel, unforgiving, and egotistical God who demanded the blood of Jesus will also demand from us, as we approach the gates of heaven, "faith in Jesus," as if it were a ticket to get into a concert. If you do not have the ticket, you cannot come in. (At this point it is interesting to remember some of the parables of Jesus, in which he depicted an entirely different "heavenly banquet," where those invited are precisely those who do not have the proper "tickets.")

What ought to be understood is that faith in Jesus is necessary and sufficient for salvation, not because it somehow opens the lock of the pearly gates, but because it allows us to join him in the struggle for a new order, in the hope for a new heaven and a new earth, whose coming is the genuine "Good News" of the gospel. Faith in Jesus is not a talisman or a ticket to be shown at the moment of the final judgment; it is the norm by which life is to be lived now. Faith in Jesus gives life, not only in the future and after death, but also now, here, in all the deaths that we are forced to endure in this life. To quote Wake again, "God, incarnate in Jesus Christ, is not so much the one who suffers and dies for us, but the one who suffers and dies with us."[8]

It is at this point that the issue of survival, which is so crucial for ethnic minorities, becomes central. Significantly, every one of the presenters at the Roundtable emphasized survival as the central issue for the people they represented, and they established a close relationship between it and salvation. For a people engaged in the awful task of survival, God's salvation must somehow involve God's intervention on their behalf. It is also at this point that we have often found the church's preaching lacking. In a moving testimony of his experience as a Japanese American in a concentration camp, Lloyd K. Wake expressed both gratitude for what other Christians have done, and a sense of frustration at the limited scope of their action:

> I've often reflected on what life would have been like in that rural town of Reedley if all the church folk would put as much energy into abolishing the sunset laws that prohibited "Negroes" from staying overnight in our town as they did in saving souls; or boycotting the one movie theatre that would not permit the Japanese to sit where the white folks sat—we sat in the balcony. Our Mennonite Brethren friends visited us while we were in the Concentration Camps in the Arizona desert during World War II. It was a compassionate act for which we were very grateful. But their religious faith never led them to speak against that injustice.[9]

For ethnic minorities, as for the ancient Israelites, survival is an everyday issue—survival both in the economic sense of having enough to live with, and in the deeper sense of having a sense of worth and of belonging. Ediberto López began his presentation with a description of "the Latino context in New York," in which he expressed his pain as a parent in that community:

> Our children would like to be Americans (White?) but are rejected by the dominant cultural system. They try to disassociate from the Latino heritage and thus become a marginal group. They are not from the dominant culture but do not want to be Latinos. The alienation is without description.[10]

For persons in such a situation, a semi-Gnostic view of salvation is very attractive, just as it was for people in similar situations in the second and third centuries. They can become Christians, be "saved," and no longer have to worry about whether they are Latinos, white, or what. They will be "saved souls"—and souls have no race.

It may be true that souls have no race; but, do they have no culture and no history? Several decades ago, philosopher José Ortega y Gasset argued against an essentialist view of human nature, saying that human nature is not a "thing," a "substance," but rather a "history." We are not something given that can be described and understood by its nature, like a rock or a planet. We are rather a history. In order to understand who a person is, we must tell that person's story. I am who I am, in part at least, because of where I was born, where I grew up, who my parents were, and a multitude of other such elements. If that is the case, what is a soul without a history, without a culture? It was very clear to us, as we sat around the Roundtable, that we were very different from one another. Some of us had grown up overseas, speaking a language that most around that table could not understand. Others had grown up in the United States, experiencing daily humiliations almost beyond description. This is who we are. We cannot be understood—we cannot even conceive of ourselves—aside from such histories and such experiences. Souls may not have race; but in a racist society they certainly are shaped by our racial and cultural identities!

Thus, for Ediberto's children—for any of our children—to be "saved" as non-ethnic souls, to be "saved" out of the need to understand themselves and claim their history and who they are, is not real salvation, but simply one more instance of alienation. Indeed, the way such "salvation" often works in practice is that the "saved" from among the ethnic minorities come to believe that, because they are saved, they must now be just like those of the dominant culture. They then buy into the values and habits of that dominant culture, without even asking whether such values and habits are compatible with the faith. Sometimes it takes years before they come to the deep realization that, converted or not, they will never be fully accepted as part of that dominant culture and society.

It may be true that souls have no race; but it is also true that conversion always takes place within a set of circumstances, and that such circumstances determine much of its content and direction. Paul's conversion implied ceasing his persecution of Christians, and joining them. For Augustine, conversion involved abandoning his career and its goals, and devoting himself first to a life of contemplation, and later to the ordained ministry of the church. For Wesley, it implied the assurance of his own salvation. For each of us, our own conversions are culturally and historically conditioned. Conversion means, not only coming to believe in Jesus Christ, but also joining in his promises—which means joining in the struggle for survival and for humanization. Conversion leads, not to peace and quiet, but to struggle and confrontation, for it is only through struggle and confrontation that the powers of evil are defeated.

What conversion has never been, and must not be, is a purely private affair, having to do only with one's relationship to God, and apart from any community of faith and of struggle. Such a "conversion," which is often peddled on our television screens, is not conversion to the Good News of Jesus Christ, which is the Good News of the Reign of God and its justice. Yet, this notion of "conversion" has often tempted the church, for it allows for the preaching of a "salvation" that has little to do with this world, and which therefore allows the oppressors to continue oppressing, and encourages the oppressed to accept their oppression.

On the other hand, as was clearly shown by the discussion around our Roundtable, those who have experienced conversion and salvation as ethnic minorities, without thereby abandoning the struggle for their survival as a people, have much to teach the rest of the church regarding the full meaning of salvation. For them—as for the Bible—salvation is not exclusively for the soul. It is not "spiritual" as opposed to "material." It is holistic and expresses God's active love for us as complete human beings, who have spiritual yearnings, but also physical and emotional needs. It is a "salvation" that clearly includes in faith a dimension of "healing"—healing for both the body and the broken relationships of our society. And vice versa, it is also a view of salvation that sees God's saving activity far beyond the religious—in medical science being able to cure a sick child, in revolutions bringing down tyranny in Eastern Europe, in South Africa, and in El Salvador, and in laws providing shelter for the homeless.

Such a holistic view of salvation should also put an end to the endless and fruitless debate regarding the relative importance of evangelism and social action. The two cannot be separated. The Good News of Jesus Christ is also the Good News that the Reign of God is at hand, that the will of God will be done on earth as it is in heaven. Christian social action must be based on this Good News, and not merely on compassion, anger, or ideological programs—although all of these certainly have a role to play. Any form of "evangelism" that invites people to believe in Jesus

Christ merely as a means to live after death limits the lordship of Christ and mutilates his gospel. We may call it "good news," but it is not the Good News of Jesus Christ. Likewise, true Christian social action is based on the vision of the coming Reign of God and on the Good News that Jesus Christ has overcome the powers of death, which oppose that Reign.

INDIVIDUALISM AND COSMOPOLITANISM

This leads to another way in which the full biblical meaning of salvation has been denied. That is the excessive emphasis on the individual. This too comes from the struggles of Christianity against Gnosticism, in the midst of the confused and confusing world of the first centuries of the Christian era. What Gnosticism promised at that point, and what made it so attractive, was personal, private salvation. It took for granted that neither the world nor society could be saved. It was, as the old saying puts it in rather sexist terms, "every man for himself." All one could do was save one's soul. At best, one could invite others to do likewise. But salvation was essentially a lonely journey of the soul, an ascension through the spheres of entrapment, until one could reach the "fullness" of eternity. Such a view of salvation was particularly attractive in a world such as that of the Hellenistic age, when people saw themselves as individuals lost in a confusing sea of humanity, with few connections that made them who they were. A Spanish peasant who had somehow become a slave, and was now living in Athens or Alexandria, with no connections defining him save those with his master, would be very attracted to such a salvation. Oddly enough, as is so often the case in this type of religiosity, this radically personal sort of salvation ended up, in many a Gnostic system, with the individual being swallowed up in the "fullness," and thus disappearing as such.

Christianity also emphasized personal salvation. It had to do so given the circumstances. From the outset, it was persecuted within its original Jewish cradle. Then, as it made its way into the Gentile world, it was persecuted even more cruelly. During the first three centuries of its existence, even at those times when it was not officially persecuted, it was regarded askance by society at large, and particularly by the opinion and image makers within that society. Therefore, converts tended to come singly, and to most of them conversion meant a break, not only with their old lives, but also with many of their old relationships.

That, however, was not the whole picture. There are in the New Testament examples of an entire household being converted (see, for instance, Acts 16:14-15 and 31-33). In any case, from the outset the community of faith, the church, had an important place in salvation. One was not simply saved into a life of private spiritual communion with the Lord. One was converted and saved into a life of communion with the Lord and with one another in the church. And, finally, the goal of salvation was seen, not as a private life everlasting, but as a resurrection into life in the Reign of God—or in the New Jerusalem—which was a new order of relationships in which there would be peace, love, justice, and abundance. Thus, although a personal conversion was the norm, this did not lead to a privatistic understanding of salvation or of the Christian life.

The legitimate emphasis on a personal decision, combined with the individualistic tendencies of the Hellenistic age, tended to make the Christian understanding of salvation increasingly privatistic. When eventually the Empire became Christian, an interesting development took place. While mass conversions soon became common, and people were expected to be Christians simply because they had been born in a Christian society, there was also a tendency to deny or downplay some of the more radical implications of Christianity for life in community. The reasons for this are obvious. The Empire was willing to become nominally Christian, as long as Christianity did not expect to change much of the manner in which imperial business was conducted. Christian leaders had to be content with preaching, and almost the only point at which they insisted on applying Christian morality to the common life was in matters having to do with sex. In economic matters, for instance, after a brief period of rather harsh preaching against the abuses of the rich and the powerful,[11] the church became content with leaving the more radical demands of the gospel to the monastics, and allowing the rest of Christians to carry on with the inordinate accumulation of wealth, with very little change from what had gone on before. Eventually, even the harsh preaching was discontinued and forgotten.

This is not the place to follow the entire history of this dialectic between the communal and the personal aspects of conversion and salvation. What is very clear is that both are important, and that Christians have tended to emphasize one or the other at various times and for various reasons. Those of us who grew up in the "mission field" know that very often missionaries emphasized the personal aspect of conversion, partly because they were in the midst of a hostile environment, but partly also because they did not understand and often did not appreciate that environment. There was a positive and a negative aspect to this preaching. On the positive side, it gave individuals the freedom to choose the gospel for themselves, often in societies where such individual choices were uncommon, and where the pressures of tradition and convention were often dehumanizing. On the negative side, it created churches that were unnecessarily alienated from the cultural roots of their members, and whose theology gave them little basis on which to reclaim those roots. As someone has said about Protestant missionary efforts in Latin America, for a century and a half those efforts were content with picking up "the loose dust on the surface" of society but never entering into the substance itself of that society and culture.

At this point it is important to draw again on the parallel situations between the first centuries of the Christian era and our own time. If there is one thing that characterizes our time it is precisely its cosmopolitanism. Cable television instantly and constantly brings us news and images from the remotest parts of the world. Within the span of half an hour, a viewer successively witnesses a revolt in the Baltic Republics, famine in Africa, industrial innovations in Japan, the struggle for freedom in South Africa, a religious service in Indonesia, a protest in front of an abortion clinic, a scandal in Washington, a particularly gory crime in New Zealand, highlights from a football game in the Midwest, "news" from Hollywood, and the weather—all interspersed with commercials for products from all over the world! Stay tuned for another half hour, and witness the same thing all over again!

Gone are—if they ever existed—the old certainties of the small community where each person had a place, and everyone went to church on Sunday morning. Nostalgia for such certainties is exploited by Madison Avenue and by politicians, but we all know that such times will not return. We live in a cosmopolitan age, with all its excitement, but also with all its fears. And also with the unavoidable questions regarding one's identity in such a vast, varied, and confusing sea of humanity and human experience.

In this country, various groups react to this situation in different ways. The question of identity, which has traditionally been a difficult one for ethnic minorities and especially for their children, has also become difficult for the dominant group. I often remember an occasion at a Greek restaurant, when the waitress asked me if I was Greek. I responded that I was not Greek, but Cuban, and then asked her what she was. After a long pause, she responded: "I guess I am nothing!" I had an identity I could name, even though it also identified me as an outsider to the culture. She, an insider, had no such identity.

For those in the dominant group in this country, increasingly at a loss as to their identity because they feel cast asea in a threateningly cosmopolitan world, Gnostic or semi-Gnostic views of salvation are particularly appealing. They are also appealing for those in the same culture who have become so sated with material things and security that the normal struggles of most of humankind no longer hold any appeal. The purely spiritualistic and individualistic view of salvation allows such people to consider themselves religious without drastically changing their life-styles—much less questioning the social order that has given them so many material advantages. It also provides a sense of meaning that does not threaten the "meanings" of the present order.

The same understanding of salvation has been proclaimed and even peddled among ethnic minorities. Some do find it attractive, for reasons similar to those already stated which are true for whites. The children of immigrants whom Ediberto López mentions in his paper, who are hoping and seeking to become assimilated into the wider society, are often attracted by this sort of religiosity, which, at least in theory, puts them on a par with those of the dominant group, and at the same time excuses them from joining in the struggles of their ethnic group.[12]

Still, ethnic minorities in this country have by and large come to a different understanding of salvation. In this respect, African American Christians have traditionally taken the lead. From the times of slavery, when spirituals combined the celebration of life eternal with the yearning for physical freedom, to the time of the Civil Rights struggle, when they mobilized themselves and the entire nation for communal salvation, African American Christians have shown that they understood salvation in terms broader than those they had been taught. Many of those who first taught them Christianity told them that, if they believed and behaved, they would go to heaven, and that therefore they should each be concerned above all for their own individual and spiritual salvation. Yet for African Americans salvation was much more than purely spiritual and individual, no matter what white evangelists preached. In this respect, as all the foregoing has amply shown, they were closer to scriptural Christianity than were those who taught a privatistic and spiritualistic religion.

The same is true, in varying degrees, of various other ethnic groups. We have all been taught a doctrine of salvation that is more Gnostic than biblical. In each of our groups there are many who find such a doctrine safe and comforting. Yet, there are also increasing numbers who are coming to a wider understanding of salvation, one that includes not only life after death, but also struggle for survival both as individuals and as groups. As we do so, it seems to us that we are also coming to a clearer understanding of what the Bible means by salvation—an understanding that may be a significant contribution to the church at large.

PIE IN THE SKY

Whenever one makes the points stated here, inevitably someone asks, Does that mean that you no longer believe in life after death? Such a question comes from a false dichotomy, itself the result of the Gnostic view of salvation and a reaction to it. The Gnostic view of salvation limits it to the salvation of the soul, made effective mostly after death. In reaction, many liberals have held that the expectation of life after death, "pie in the sky," is counterproductive to the struggle for justice and survival in this world. Yet the liberal tenet that the hope of life after death leads to social passivity is not true. History shows that, on the contrary, the most actively revolutionary groups within Christianity have had a strong eschatological expectation, and an equally strong conviction of life after death. What is indeed conducive to resignation and passivity is not the expectation of life after death, but the *Gnostic* understanding of such expectation.

On the other hand, the notion of "pie in the sky," if properly understood, is not all that bad. First of all, it raises the question of justice here and now. If there is to be pie in the sky, that means that it is not wrong to wish for pie. If God promises pie, how come the present social order gives some all the pie and others all the hunger? If God promises pie in the sky, clearly there is something wrong with earth, and God's will is not being done "on earth as it is in heaven." One reason why those Christians with the most vivid eschatological expectations have usually been also the most radically revolutionary is precisely that the Reign of God, with its peace, justice, and abundance, acts as a judgment upon the orders and the disorders of human society.

Second, the firm conviction of life after death deprives the oppressors of their ultimate tool of control, the fear of death. If death has the last word, those who have the power to kill also have the last word. To a lesser degree, those who have the power to employ and to fire, to promote and to demote, also have great power, for they can control this life, and we have no other. If, on the other hand, even death will not separate us from the love of Christ, who himself is victor over the powers of death, we can risk life, employment, and physical well-being for the sake of justice and God's reign.

Thus, salvation has to do with life after death, but also with life before death.[13] As she prepared her paper for presentation, Evelene Sombrero went about asking several persons at random, among her Navajo friends, about the meaning of the terms "salvation, struggle, survival," and then told us: "I've finally come to the conclusion that these three things are what we do every day."[14] Salvation does not have to wait for death to occur, for as Lloyd Wake stated, this salvation which carries on beyond the grave

> goes far beyond any personal salvation (saving my skin). It has to do with being delivered (liberated) from a sense of victimization, second class citizenship, and powerlessness. Salvation has to do with possessing or repossessing land, being delivered from segregated schools . . . and freedom to exercise one's conscience.[15]

99

CHAPTER SIX

VISIONS OF THE CHURCH

COMMITMENT AND ALIENATION

T he 1990 session of the Roundtable turned its attention to the doctrine of the church. It soon became clear that in a very real sense we were talking about ourselves, and yet we were also speaking about something "out there," almost as if it were an alien reality that we were examining from outside. The tone was one of profound commitment to the church, and of equally profound distrust of it. Yet these two elements—commitment and distrust, participation and alienation, love and hostility—did not cancel each other out. Our distrust of the church did not diminish our commitment to it, nor did our commitment ease our distrust. Therefore, in order to understand our visions of the church we must begin by examining these two poles of our relationship to it.

To understand the depth of the commitment of ethnic minorities to the church it is necessary to recognize the role of the church in each of our communities. In this regard, much has been said and written about the role of the black church. One of the ways in which the institution of slavery sought to perpetuate itself, and to avoid the specter of massive rebellion, was the systematic destruction of African traditions and identity. Although much remained, many of the traditional expressions of African identity were suppressed. In that situation, the church became for many a new basis on which to create an African American identity—as E. Franklin Frazier has said, "a nation within a nation." In a society where practically every other avenue was closed to people of African descent, the church became the matrix in which black leaders were formed, and the surroundings from which they drew their support, as became evident at the height of the Civil Rights movement.

Among Native Americans, on the other hand, the church has traditionally played a very different role. It was part of an invading culture, which sought to supplant all that was traditional, often by means of violent imposition. As Seneca United Methodist minister Marvin B. Abrams says, "The result has been that many accepted the new faith, and consciously spurned their religious and cultural traditions and even language. However, there were others who resisted Christianity and were faithful to their sacred teachings and rituals. These two extremes have always existed."[1] Abrams himself was forbidden by his grandmother from attending the traditional "naming ceremony" at the longhouse, and thus lived most of his adult life without a traditional Seneca name. What Native Americans were forced to abandon in order to join the church was not just one or two religious ceremonies and beliefs, quite apart from the rest of their lives. What from the perspective of the missionaries were discrete "pagan" elements in "Indian" culture, were in fact part of the very fiber of that culture. Thus, when Native Americans, for whatever reason, joined the church, they also had to abandon much of their culture and traditions. This is illustrated in a story told in his *Autobiography* by Duane Porter, a Chippewa clergyman. He and other Christians had borrowed the grand medicine lodge in a village, when the following occurred:

> We gathered together a company of converts and went inside the lodge, took down all the wooden images of birds and animals, carried out the drum and threw all these things in a pile. Soon many of the old pagan Indians came up the hill with their little drums, medicine bags, skins of small animals used in the medicine lodge ceremony and threw them also on the pile. We then walked around the lodge hall singing, "Nearer My God to Thee." Some young brave touched a match to the pile of pagan relics and a great fire consumed them as we stood and watched.[2]

Homer Noley comments that "even the most traditional of Natives are willing to make great sacrifices to demonstrate the integrity of their commitment."[3]

Under such conditions, constantly having to justify their church membership both to their neighbors and to themselves, Christian Native Americans were led to place the church at the very center of their life and their identity. Some of these conditions have changed in more recent times, as Native American Christian leaders are seeking to relate the gospel to their traditional roots, and as some churches are providing a forum for dialogue between Christianity and traditional religion. Yet, the consequences of that long history cannot be undone in a few years.

Among Hispanics and Asian Americans, the church has performed a very different function, for it has served both to preserve the traditional culture and language and, to a limited degree, to bridge part of the gap with the dominant culture. Puerto Ricans in New York, nostalgic for the

human and physical warmth of their island and their culture, and forced
to live in a very different environment, often gather in churches that seek
to perpetuate the music, customs, and social rituals of their homeland.
The same is true of Cubans in South Florida, Vietnamese in Houston,
Koreans in Chicago, and Chinese in California. As a result, the church
plays a very important role in the life of such people, for it is the vehicle
and expression, not only of their faith, but also of their cultural identity.
Sometimes, the role of the church as a center for cultural identity—and as
a service agent for ethnic minorities—even surpasses its role as a faith
community. Such is the case of the community described by Chinese
American pastor Timothy Ting:

> The church in an immigrant community has a much more complex role
> than it does in a more stable and settled society. People come to church not
> because of religious reasons. Many people have no faith at all, yet they come
> merely because they are longing for relationship and want to meet and to be
> associated with their own race. They come for social purposes.[4]

Although many readers will interpret these words of Pastor Ting in a
negative way, that is not the way they were meant, nor the way they were
interpreted in the subsequent discussion. On the contrary, what they
mean is that God is active in the various longings and needs that bring
people to church; that "social purposes" are part of God's overarching
purposes for humanity.

To this is added a second role for many of these churches: They serve as
a partial bridge between minorities and the dominant culture. Christian
members of various immigrant groups have traditionally found that the
only thing they had in common with the dominant culture was their profession of faith. This is changing, as institutional Christianity becomes ever
less dominant among American whites. Yet it is still true that in many parts
of the United States the one point of social contact and commonality that
recent immigrants can establish with society at large is their profession of
Christianity.

Furthermore, all of us agreed on the crucial and constructive role that
churches play in our communities. People whose humanity is often
denied in society at large—and for whom the memory of slavery, segre-
gation, exile, and refugee camp is very vivid—find in the church an
atmosphere that not only welcomes them, but grants them full citizenship. If our people have an experience of deliverance, it is often through
worship that such an experience is experienced and expressed. The
churches are the most stable institutions in most of our poorest neigh-
borhoods, and the only ones that remain there when public or private
funding falters. They have been and still are the place where most
autochthonous ethnic minority leadership is trained, where our people

learn about conflict management, democratic and parliamentary procedures, and so forth.

All of this means that the church is very important for all of these
groups, and hence the commitment to it that characterizes ethnic minority Christians—a commitment that often implies attending services and
church meetings with a frequency that whites find astonishing!

Yet the role of the church as a preserver of cultural identity also has its
problems. Members of immigrant minority cultures, especially the
elderly, have very little influence on most of the institutions affecting
their lives—government, schools, banks, and so on. The one exception is
the church. Here they can determine the program, activities, and other
agenda. In many cases this older generation, concerned that the young
are losing their traditional culture, uses the church to counterbalance
outside influences by teaching the language, customs, and history. This
can have both positive and negative effects. At a time in their lives when
many children and young people are seeking to be as much like their
peers as possible, their parents and their church insist on making them
different. For many, the use of the "old" language seems an imposition.
In such cases the conflict between generations, which is already serious in
many immigrant groups, is exacerbated, and the church is placed at the
very center of that conflict. In the end, many among the young vent their
resentment against that situation by leaving the church as soon as they
are old enough to do so. That is one of the reasons why many among the
ethnic minorities feel alienated from the church. On the positive side,
when programs stressing cultural identity are conducted with wisdom and
understanding, they help the younger generation understand why they
are different from their white, only-English-speaking peers, and to be
proud of their identity.

The reasons for the sense of alienation from the church, however, go
much farther than that. They have to do with the manner in which the
church at large has dealt with minorities and with the issues that most concern us. Again, it is important to insist that this sense of alienation in no
way diminishes our commitment to and love for the church. As an illustra-
tion of this point, in his presentation before the Roundtable, William B.
McClain underscored the profound sense of gratitude for the Methodist
church even among those black leaders who felt compelled to leave it.
Among others, he quoted Richard Allen, founder of the African
Methodist Episcopal Church: "I cannot be anything but a Methodist, as I
was born and awakened under them."[5] What Allen meant, and many
other African American religious leaders have reaffirmed, was that, even
though the church's racism had forced him to leave it, he still loved it!

The reasons why many ethnic minority persons feel alienated from the
church are similar to those that led Allen to leave the Methodist church.

They have to do with a sense of not belonging, or of having to become like the majority in order to belong. As Lloyd K. Wake put it,

> In the church, assimilation and absorption has been the *modus operandi*— i.e., the minority is absorbed by the majority, the east assimilated by the west, the young into the old, the powerless into the powerful.[6]

Ethnic minorities do acknowledge that the churches in general, and The United Methodist Church in particular, have made great strides in recent decades on the task of correcting institutional racial injustice within the church. In his paper, McClain outlines some of this progress:

> In 1965 there were eight newly appointed black superintendents of districts whose churches were mostly white. That was big news in 1965 and a real surprise to most black United Methodists. By 1978 the number had climbed to 39, and in 1988, it was more than 60.
>
> In the area of the General Conference delegates there was a dramatic change. In 1964 the number elected from newly merged conferences was 14. A quadrennium later the figure rose to 24. At the 1988 General Conference the number was higher than was true in the days of the all-black Central Jurisdiction. General board leadership at the top level dramatically increased after 1968 and concerted efforts of Black Methodists for Church Renewal. From 1969 to 1984 executive posts went from 50 to 110.[7]

In spite of such progress, however, there is still much to be done before the feeling of alienation can begin to be assuaged. More concretely, part of the discussion at the Roundtable had to do with what we termed the "quadrilateral of oppression"—obviously a not-so-veiled reference to the more traditional Methodist "Quadrilateral." This quadrilateral of oppression includes *gender, class, culture,* and *race.*[8] All four of these are employed as means of oppression, often playing one against the other. Thus, for instance, it is quite common for ethnic minority churches to protest racial oppression, while in their midst women are kept out of decision-making positions. Likewise, it is not uncommon for white women to gather for a meal at church to discuss issues of women's liberation, while the meal itself is being prepared in the kitchen by minority women whose wages leave much to be desired.

The matter of class is particularly important when it comes to the life of the church. Indeed, some at the Roundtable posed the question of whether the statistics cited by McClain, regarding the number of black district superintendents, bishops, board and agency executives, and others, did not simply accept the existing pyramidal view of the church, and buy into it. Should our goal be to have more ethnic minorities in positions of power within the church, or should it be rather to change the very nature and exercise of power in the church? This is only one of many questions raised when the issue of class is introduced in the discussion. In this regard, the crucial question is, Have our churches (and more concretely, The United Methodist Church) so organized themselves as to practically exclude the poor, no matter what their race, culture, or gender?

We are all agreed that racism is a great evil, and one that must be excised from church and society. Yet, in order to counteract racism, we must be aware of its connections with classism—for instance, that racism is often used by the dominant classes in order to convince poor whites that they are not oppressed and should therefore support the whites who in fact exploit them.

Along these lines, Daniel Rodríguez pointed out that in Latin America Protestant Christianity, at least in its "mainline" expression, has become captive to the existing social order:

> At the beginning large numbers joined the churches of mainline Protestantism, but very soon its message of hope was reduced to those who could climb the social ladder in highly stratified neocolonial societies. Mainline Protestant Christianity in Latin America and the Caribbean became more the church with a middle class ideology and social structure. Many of the poor were attracted to it; but it did not become the church of the poor.[9]

THE ECCLESIOLOGY OF CHRISTENDOM

This leads to the main point at which many of us are dissatisfied with the church, and have come to feel alienated from it: Even in the United States, with its theoretical and legal separation between church and state, the operating ecclesiology is essentially one of "Christendom." Rodríguez' paper pointed out that, although we are well aware of the "old Spanish-Mexican Christendom," which was Catholic, we are not quite so ready to see similar dimensions in the "Anglo-American Christendom," which is Protestant. Clearly, we do not have here a situation where a single church or denomination is equated with society, as in traditional Christendom. But we do have a situation where the church—at least the church of "mainline" Protestantism—tends to obscure the distance between its own message and values and the values of society at large.[10] The dominant vision here is one of a "Christian civilization," in which, although it is acknowledged that one's civilization must still be corrected, it is also taken for granted that one's culture is more Christian than the rest. When that happens, the institutional self-interest of the church and the interests of the status quo become united and confused in an unholy alliance. This in turn makes the church appear irrelevant to those who do not benefit from the status quo, and whose daily struggles the church seems to ignore. As Cain H. Felder put it:

> Despite the many impressive cathedrals of Europe and America, and the highly visible, vocal and commercial nature of so much of American religiosity, many people perceive the Church as irrelevant to the on-going, vital concerns of daily life. For these, the Church has become too closely identified with national culture and the economic-political establishment. The realities of the church's own institutional self-interest and role as conservator of socio-cultural values have, perhaps unwittingly, caused her to function almost as priest—at times even royal priest—to the *status quo,* while tending to forget her call to prophetic witness.[11]

A clear example of the consequences of this view, and how it confuses its own traditions with Christian values, was pointed out by Marvin Abrams. According to Abrams, "Missionaries, working hand in hand with the government, demanded that each Indian family find meaning in being a self-sufficient and independent economic unit." In so doing, these missionaries were obviously convinced that they were bringing their converts closer to Christian standards, yet, as Abrams says, "This was at odds with the native values of generosity, hospitality, and communal interdependence." [12] He could easily have gone on and pointed out what was clearly implicit in his comments, namely, that at least in this respect the Native American "pagans" were closer to the Christian understanding of life than were the missionaries seeking to convert them. What was happening was simply that these missionaries, coming as they did from a "Christian culture," took for granted that wherever that culture differed from that of the Native Americans the former was to be preferred as being closer to the Christian ideal.[13] Such is the result of the "ecclesiology of Christendom"—or, to use a term more widely used nowadays, of "civil religion." The outcome is what Abrams calls a "historical mistrust" of the church on the part, not only of Native Americans, but also of most others who do not share the culture the "ecclesiology of Christendom" identifies with the church. Speaking of the community he serves in Southern California, in which there are approximately one hundred and fifty tribes represented, Abrams says:

> There are many who have reservations about the church in this particular American Indian community. Someone called this, and I tend to agree with them, historical mistrust. Many Native Americans have come to our church in Los Angeles, and say that this is a "white man's" church. This statement is not without some truth. Many missionaries went to "Indian Country" with, I am sure, noble intentions. However, they were more intent on civilizing the native American, than in bringing them into the presence of God.[14]

One wonders whether the missionaries to whom Abrams alludes did see a difference between preaching the gospel and "civilizing" the Native Americans. Most probably, they were able to recognize that distinction in theory but could not apply it in practice. Such is precisely the problem with a Christianity that becomes too closely identified with the structures and expectations of society: not being able to see the difference between those structures and expectations and the genuine demands of the gospel, and thus coming to the conclusion that anyone and anything that does not conform to the mores and standards prescribed by the dominant society is of necessity pagan. The "ecclesiology of Christendom," as Rodríguez depicted it, is characterized precisely by this confusion of Christianity and culture.

That very word, "pagan," has an interesting history which illustrates the point. Originally, *paganus* referred to things and people who were rustic, belonging to the countryside or the village as opposed to the city. It also meant "civilian" in contrast to "military." It was in the latter sense that Christians first used it to refer to those who did not belong to the church—that is, to the "army of Christ."[15] The term, however, did not become a common way to refer to non-Christians until late in the fourth century, after the Roman Empire had become Christian. By then Christianity was rapidly becoming the religion of the dominant classes, and the old religion was pejoratively dubbed "pagan" to indicate that it was the faith of rustic, ignorant peasants. In contrast to such people, Christians were "civilized"—that is, cultured, "citified." Thus, the connection between "civilization" and Christianity on the one hand, and "uncivilized" or "pagan" on the other, is a by-product of the ecclesiology of Christendom, which began flourishing precisely in the fourth century.

In the Western Hemisphere, in missions among the Native Americans to whom Abrams refers, "pagan" came to mean, not so much "rustic" or "peasant," as "savage." Therefore, the

> process of Christianizing became coincident with the process of educating or civilizing. Since the Indians were by definition "savages," Christianizing them meant destroying their Indianness and transforming them into whites of a darker hue.[16]

It is thus that the "ecclesiology of Christendom" understands the mission of the church, even to this day.

In imitation of the society in which it was formed, this ecclesiology understands the church in terms of a pyramidal, hierarchical, male-dominated institution. When the church was joined to the Empire, it began imitating the structures and practices of the Empire and its court, not only in matters of worship, but also in matters of structure. Even the word "diocese," which today is a purely ecclesiastical term, originally referred to an administrative district in the Roman Empire. In this process, the church organized itself in a manner similar to that in which the imperial army and administration were organized. At first, some exceptionally powerful laymen, such as Emperor Constantine, held great authority in the church; but the system was rapidly made clerical, particularly in the Latin-speaking western portion of Europe. Eventually, the laity was practically excluded from all decision making in the life of the church—except when a particularly powerful ruler was able to make his or her wish obeyed. The Reformation did restore power and authority to the laity, on the basis of the "priesthood of all believers." But in truth it generally accepted the structures of power that existed in society at large, giving authority in the church to the same people who had authority in that society—in the sixteenth century, mostly noblemen, and, as modern capitalism emerged, rich entrepreneurs and the managerial class. Since ethnic minorities—and women—have seldom been represented among such people, they have had and still have very little say in the manner in which the church conducts its business. For this reason, when discussing the manner in which Western nations and civilization have plundered the rest of the world, Stephen Kim declared that "the Church itself seems to be one more such plunderer, if we judge by the mission programs of the majority of the churches."[17] And Cain Felder agreed: "The realities of the church's own institutional self-interest and role as conservator of socio-cultural values have, perhaps unwittingly, caused her to function almost as priest—at times even royal priest—to the *status quo,* while tending to forget her call to prophetic witness."[18]

It is over against such ecclesiology that participants in the Roundtable expressed a profound sense of alienation. The comment was made that in The United Methodist Church, as well as in other denominations, there is an elite that knows how to "work" the church, while the majority do not—and it was also said, somewhat tongue-in-cheek, that when too many people begin to understand how the church functions, it is time to restructure! Above all, the concern was raised that, following the principles of organization applied in corporations and in society at large, the church has organized itself in such a way that the rich and powerful churches—most of which have very few ethnic minority members—continue growing rich and powerful, while the smaller churches must struggle along. When it comes to the system of appointing pastors, the larger the church, the more democratic the system becomes; and the smaller the church, the more feudalistic. And, when the proper balance of "freedom and order" was discussed, someone declared that the problem is that the large churches get most of the freedom, and the smaller ones get most of the order! The sense of alienation in these comments should be obvious.

ECCLESIOLOGY AND ESCHATOLOGY

From that discussion, and as one reads the papers presented at the 1990 session of the Roundtable, it becomes apparent that the eschatological dimension of ecclesiology is crucial if one is to understand the way in which ethnic minorities look at the church. Rodríguez expressed it thus: "The church represents the first fruits of that relation which Christ wants to establish with all humanity. The community of believers is the wedge that helps to open the spring of a new creation." [19] McClain spoke of a "rehearsing church" in which "we are preparing to live in the Kingdom." [20] What he meant by this was not a church that spends its time looking at heaven, but rather a church that, on the basis of its vision of the Reign of God, works on earth as those who truly anticipate that Reign. And Abrams, in an implicit reference to the sweatlodge experience of universal kinship, spoke of the community of faith as grounded in God's promise "to sustain the building of a world in which we are all relatives." [21]

Evidently, part of the driving force for this eschatological emphasis is the sense that the present world is not as it should be. For obvious reasons, this feeling tends to be stronger among minorities, whom the present order often bemeans and oppresses, than among those of the dominant race and culture. If my people and I are not allowed to take our proper place within this world and society, I will find great solace in views that affirm that God's will and God's promised order are very different, and that this will and those promises are to be used to judge the present order. Thus arises the eschatological ecclesiology that seemed to be a common theme in our Roundtable discussions on the nature of the church.

In the New Testament, the church is much more than a group of people who get together periodically to worship God and to receive spiritual nourishment. It is much more than an institution whose purpose is to invite others to believe, and to join them in doing good works. It certainly is much more than a service station where we go to have our tank filled for the rest of the week!

In the New Testament, the church is described with very radical images—images which have become so common to us that we often miss their radicality. In his presentation, following the lead of Orlando Costas, Daniel Rodríguez made use of several of these images, which are worth exploring further. [22]

The first such image is that of the church as people of God, for which the passage most often quoted is I Peter 2:9-10:

> But you are a chosen race, a royal priesthood, a holy nation, God's own people, in order that you may proclaim the mighty acts of him who called you out of darkness into his marvelous light.
> Once you were not a people,
> > but now you are God's people;
> > once you had not received mercy,
> > but now you have received mercy.

There are many elements in this passage that would be worthy of attention. In the context of our discussion here, what stands out is the paradoxical notion that, in the midst of a world divided by racism, God has created still another race! This theme was picked up by Aristides, one of the earliest Christians who wrote in defense of their faith against those who mocked and persecuted it. According to Aristides, there are "barbarians," Greeks, Jews, and, now, Christians.[23] We may dislike such notions, and particularly the very idea of a "chosen race," to the point of refusing to deal with a text such as this, for we are well aware of the evil that claims of "chosenness" have brought upon the world, even in our own twentieth century.

For that reason it is important that we clarify the nature and purpose of this chosenness: It is neither born out of virtue, nor does it lead to privilege.

It is not born out of virtue. In another well-known passage, which Rodríguez also quotes, Paul makes this clear:

> Consider your own call, brothers and sisters: not many of you were wise by human standards, not many were powerful, not many were of noble birth. But God chose what is foolish in the world to shame the wise; God chose what is weak in the world to shame the strong; God chose what is low and despised in the world, things that are not, to reduce to nothing things that are. (I Cor. 1:26-28)

This new people, this new race, is chosen, not because it has anything special, but precisely because it does not. It cannot boast of any wisdom, or power, or virtue of its own, by reason of which it has been chosen. On the contrary, it has been chosen, if for any reason at all, precisely because of its powerlessness, its folly, its nothingness.

And it has been chosen with a purpose, which is not one of privilege, or the aggrandizement of the chosen race. In the passage of I Peter, the purpose is "that you may proclaim the mighty acts of him who called you out of darkness into his marvelous light." In the passage from Corinthians, it is "to reduce to nothing things that are." These are not two different things, but two perspectives on the same reality. To be brought from darkness into marvelous light does not mean simply to be intellectually illumined, to be brought out of ignorance, or to be "converted." It means rather to be brought out of non-being: "Once you were not a people, but now you are God's people." The "mighty acts" of the One who has performed this are precisely the acts of the One who chooses "things that are not, to reduce to nothing things that are." And this in itself is an eschatological statement. The One who has promised that "the first shall be last" has chosen things that are not, "to reduce to nothing things that are."

In regard to races and racism, it is important to point out that God creates a "chosen race." This race is chosen, not because of its great cultural traditions, architectural marvels, or literary masterpieces, but precisely in order to shame any race that considers itself superior on the basis of such things. And its task is "to reduce to nothing things that are." In the context of the passage, this does not mean that things that exist are to be annihilated or obliterated. What it means is that those who consider themselves "something" will be shown to be "nothing," and that this will be done precisely by those "nobodies" whom God has made "somebodies." Likewise, when it comes to cultures and races, this does not mean that they shall be obliterated, but that they shall be put in their proper place, as contributors to that vast, all-encompassing, "catholic" reality which God's shalom envisions. (And it is important to remember at this point that "catholic" does not mean "uniform," or all blended together into a single "melting pot," but rather an all-encompassing unity in which all bring their varied gifts, and all receive and learn from one another.)

This is the vision of the church expressed by William McClain:

> . . . to become a truly inclusive church—the people of God, reflecting the colors of the rainbow as they gather in whatever place—and not simply at national meetings; to be a pluralistic church that recognizes our God-given uniqueness, but which embraces our Christ-given oneness; to be a church able to achieve internally, and model internationally, racial empowerment, justice and inclusiveness. In becoming that rehearsing church, we are preparing to live in the Kingdom. But in the process of solving a problem of such magnitude and meeting the challenge of such a common task, black and white Methodists and those of all hues in between these colors may well rediscover that larger community of interest they knew when there was neither Jew nor Greek, neither white nor black, but just a simple fellowship of believers in Jesus Christ who could gather around a common meal to say or sing: "Christ has died, Christ is risen, Christ will come again."[24]

The image of the church as the body of Christ has similar dimensions. In our modern, pragmatic society, we tend to reduce the significance of this image to its functional aspects: The church is the body of Christ, because it is through the church that Christ acts in the world today. And

111

we even carry this image so far as to declare, in opposition to all that Scripture tells us, that "he has no feet but our feet."

That, however, is not the only meaning of this image in the New Testament. In the New Testament, the church is the body of Christ in eschatological as well as in functional terms—indeed, if one understands eschatology and function correctly, the two are one. The church is the body of Christ because Christ, the New Adam, is the head of the new creation, and the church is its first fruits. Christ is the head of the church; but it is also true that God's plan is "to gather up all things under Christ, as under one head" (Eph. 1:10).[25] Thus, to say that the church is the body of Christ is to say, among other things, that it is the body that lives, even now, by the power of his resurrection. As Paul put it, precisely because we are the body of Christ, "you have died, and your life is hidden with Christ in God. When Christ who is your life is revealed, then you also will be revealed with him in glory" (Col. 3:3-4).

There is another meaning to the image of the church as the body of Christ. This is the image of a body in which different members perform different functions, and therefore all are to be affirmed, each in its own function—another dimension of what I have discussed earlier under the title "catholicity." This appears most clearly in I Corinthians 12:12-31. There Paul makes the argument that there is a variety of gifts of the Spirit, and that one who has a particular gift cannot argue that one who has a different gift does not belong to the body, just as the foot cannot say to the hand that it is not of the body. This passage is well known, and is often quoted in settings where the diversity which exists within the church is most obvious, such as ecumenical gatherings, meetings having to do with racial and cultural pluralism, and so on.

There is, however, a part of this passage that is usually ignored or glossed over, and which shows the connection between this passage and the words of Jesus, that "the last shall be first." Paul says, not simply that all are equal and should be treated equally, but also that in this particular body, care must be taken to correct existing inequities:

> The members of the body that seem to be weaker are indispensable, and those members of the body that we think less honorable we clothe with greater honor, and our less respectable members are treated with greater respect; whereas our more respectable members do not need this. But God has so arranged the body, giving the greater honor to the inferior member.
>
> (I Cor. 12:22-24)

When we say that the church is the body of Christ, what we mean is not simply that it does Christ's work; or that in it everyone has a place; or that, because we are his body, we will conquer death just as he has conquered. We are saying all of this; but we are saying also that in this particular body those whom the world treats with least honor must be given the place of honor.

It is at this point that the eschatological nature of the church must be clear. If the church is simply an institution seeking to do Christ's work in the world by means of the same instruments and procedures that the world uses, then it must be run by those who have worldly power. One is reminded of a story in Acts 8, about a man in Samaria named Simon whose power and prestige were so great that people said of him, "This man is that power of God which is called great." According to the story, Simon was converted by Philip's preaching, and was baptized; but he then wished to buy from the apostles the power to confer the Spirit by the laying on of hands. To this proposal, Peter replied: "Your silver perish with you, because you thought you could obtain God's gift with money!" Why is Peter so upset? Didn't he see how much good he could do with Simon's money? Why does he dare so to insult Philip's star convert and most valuable fundraising prospect? Because the very nature of the church would be perverted by Simon's proposal. Instead of being the eschatological body of Christ, living by the power of the resurrected, and announcing by its very life the new life that is in Jesus Christ, it would have become one more social club, where power and prestige are recognized, where the first are first, the last are last, everyone (that is, everyone who can afford it) has a good time, and nothing has changed.

Jesus himself provided an alternative ecclesiology, and did it quite clearly, when two of his disciples asked for special privileges:

> You know that among the Gentiles those whom they recognize as their rulers lord it over them, and their great ones are tyrants over them. But it is not so among you; but whoever wishes to become great among you must be your servant, and whoever wishes to be first among you must be slave of all.
> (Mark 10:42-44)

Furthermore, this is not an isolated passage, but a clear explanation of what has taken place immediately before in the Gospel. In Mark 10:13-16, Jesus comes to the defense of little children. He does this, not as our romanticizing modern interpretations would say, because they are cute or because they are innocent, but because in that society they were not considered to be of much worth. And immediately after that, when a rich man comes to him for a professional consultation about salvation, Jesus concludes with words that our modern churches seldom take seriously: "How hard it will be for those who have wealth to enter the kingdom of God!" No wonder then that Jesus was crucified, and that, in Mark 9, he warned his disciples that any who would truly follow him would also suffer a similar fate! He was not about to form a new religious club, where the good and the holy and the pure and the respectable and the rich would have

113

the first seats. He was rather proposing a subversion of that entire order, and setting up an entirely different one: the church!

Thus we come back to the deep sense of both commitment and alienation that was expressed throughout the deliberations of the Roundtable. The message the church proclaims reaches our people, and draws from them a profound sense of commitment. For many of them, their conversion to Christianity has brought about painful breaks with family, friends, and tradition. At the same time, we are convinced that the Christian message provides great and unequaled hope for precisely those families, friends, and traditions. Yet we do not often see the church living and structuring its life by that hope which it proclaims. Our people are generally powerless, and have been drawn to the gospel message of empowerment; yet when we look at the principal denominations we often see a church in which power is used to control rather than to empower the weak, and in which the first remain first, while the last must be content with crumbs under the table, with token representatives and small adjustments.

What can we say to all this? In our Roundtable, and hopefully in this book, we have attempted to show that ethnic minorities, upon whom the church has traditionally looked primarily as objects of mission, do have much to contribute to the church at large as well as to its understanding of the gospel. Beyond that, perhaps our most important contribution is to raise again the cry: Let the church be the church! Let the church be the people of God, a people chosen, not for their virtue, power, or wisdom, but by the greater virtue, power, and wisdom of God. Let the church be the body of Christ, a body in which the weaker and seemingly less honorable members are dressed with greater honor. Let the church be the church!

CHAPTER SEVEN

BY THE POWER OF THE SPIRIT

T he reader who has had the patience to follow this book to this point is well aware that what we are speaking of is no mean enterprise. Indeed, we are speaking of a general reformation of the church and its theology, and in particular of the way in which they reflect—or rather do not reflect—the catholicity of the church and of the gospel. If our perceptions are correct, much of what passes for traditional theology is in reality the result of the alliance between the church and the power structures of society. And, if what was said in the last chapter about the church is also correct, such an alliance is no less than a corruption of the very essence of the church, which by nature is the church of the last and the least. This means that we are caught between the need to reform the church and the realization that such reformation goes against the power structures of our day.

We know that we are not equal to the task, and sometimes we are not even certain that we really wish to undertake it. Yet, as was said in the very first chapter, God has never called the church to easy tasks.

How, then, dare we hope? We dare hope because the life and obedience of the church do not ultimately depend on us, but on the power of the Spirit. In the Creed, the clause on the church, "I believe in the Holy Catholic Church," appropriately appears under the greater heading: "I believe in the Holy Spirit." We believe in the church, we believe that it will be reformed to its true nature, not because we trust our own programs of reformation, and even less because we trust its structures and committees, but because we trust in the Holy Spirit.

The Holy Spirit is the *vinculum amoris*—the bond of love—which binds the church together. Were it not for the Spirit, the church would not have the slightest chance of being truly catholic—that is, of embracing within itself the vast pluralism of the human race. With the Spirit, the church has

115

no other option but to do so—for it was the Spirit who on that day of Pentecost made the message heard in a multitude of tongues, thus inviting all, near and far, to join God's action in the world.

The Holy Spirit is the first fruits—perhaps even better, the down payment—of the Reign of God. As Paul puts it in Romans 8, we groan in travail with the whole of creation, waiting for the day when creation itself will be free from its bondage. Meanwhile, we have the first fruits of the Spirit, and it is because of this gauge of God's promises that we are able to live in hope even as we share in the labor pains of creation.

Therefore, we do not despair, but rather we continue the struggle in hope. Now and then, thanks be to God, we are given a glimpse of the new order God has promised. Here and there, in an exceptional act of love, in an unexpected liberation, we are given those glimpses which we—poor, faithless creatures that we are—need in order to continue the struggle. And continue the struggle we shall—not because we are brave or firm, but because the Holy Spirit of God will not allow us to do otherwise.

As part of this struggle, we shall continue the work of the Roundtable. In the next cycle of our conversations, we shall be seeking for ways to be more inclusive, not only in our composition, but also in our very procedures. We hope to ask new questions, with new interlocutors, and in new ways.

Yet what is important is not that a few of us continue the dialogue, but rather that all of us, as children of the same Parent, undertake the dialogue; that we seek to make effective the love we profess; that we promote among all peoples the discovery which did not take place five hundred years ago, but must take place now if we are to survive.

We can do it; we shall do it, by the power of the Holy Spirit!

STATEMENT OF PURPOSE

"Uncover the Myths, Discover the Truth, Recover the Community"

The United Methodist Church is rightfully proud of its ethnic diversity. There is hardly another ecclesiastical body in the United States that can boast of such diversity of membership, both among its rank and file, and among its leadership. At the same time, this diversity has not been entirely painless. Ethnic minorities often feel that their identity and contribution have not been fully appreciated, encouraged, and received by the church at large. Some among the majority culture complain that ethnic minority concerns are often presented to them in such a way that they are made to feel guilty and experience very little that is positive in the encounter.

The Ethnic Theologians Roundtable proposes a process that will hopefully help all of us claim our identity and discover and affirm our mutual value, as well as what our several perspectives can contribute to a fuller understanding of the gospel. We are hoping that this process will result in a positive experience that can help the entire church be more truly catholic, and genuinely rejoice in that catholicity.

More specifically, we plan to direct the project toward the highly significant date, 1992. That date will mark the fifth centennial of the so-called discovery of America. There is the danger that 1992 will be the occasion for a mindless "celebration" of self-righteous myths that obscure our corporate and individual responsibility for much of the injustice in our church and society. What happened in 1492, and much of what has happened since, fell short of a true discovery. What we hope is to provide the church with some instruments to promote its own discovery of the multiplicity within itself, and in our society. Such discovery must not be based, as is too often the case, on power, prejudice, and exploitation, but on being able to receive and to rejoice in one another's gifts.

By 1992, we hope to have produced a series of written instruments to help the church—ourselves included—in that process of rediscovery. We intend for these instruments to engage the church at every level. They must include a compilation of our insight into the crucial theological themes which have always engaged the church, written in such a way as to acknowledge and receive the contribution of traditional North-Atlantic theology, and set forth what our own varied experiences and insights can contribute to a fuller understanding and living out of the gospel. We also hope that other similar materials will be produced to engage the entire church in a similar study and process—adult Sunday school materials, youth materials, worship resources, and so on. It is our dream that the entire church—or as much of it as possible—will be able to undergo this experience and study.

The next step in this process will be a meeting of ethnic minority theologians to discuss this project, refine it, and take the initial steps toward its implementation. Our present plan is that already at that first meeting, and at successive meetings until the early months of 1991, a number of crucial issues will be addressed, thus starting a dialogue that will be reflected in the final product in 1992.

Each of our annual meetings will focus on a selected number of issues (for instance, the interpretation of Scripture, Christianity and culture, the doctrine of God, the doctrine of creation, the meaning of incarnation, and so forth). There will be a full discussion of each of these issues, with written papers and responses, as well as an open forum. The results will be circulated, so that the dialogue on these issues continues until materials are brought together, not as a compilation of papers and responses, but as a coherent whole in which the essence and results of our dialogue are expounded in such a way that readers can join in it.

LIST OF PRESENTATIONS AT THE ROUNDTABLE

Salvation, Survival, Struggle:
   A Native American Reflection ....*Evelene Sombrero*
Salvation, Struggle, and Survival:
   An Asian-American Reflection..*Lloyd K. Wake*
Salvation, Struggle, and Survival: A Latino Approach ....*Ediberto López*

SESSION OF 1990

Lead Us Now to Make New History:
   An African-American Perspective ....*William B. McClain*
Community of Faith: The Sacred Circle of Life.
   A Native American Perspective..................................*Marvin B. Abrams*
The Church as a Community of Faith:
   An Asian American Perspective ....*Timothy Ting*
Historical Perspective of Latino Ecclesiologies......*Daniel R. Rodríguez-Díaz*

NOTES

CHAPTER 1: INTRODUCTION

1. Leonard Little Finger, quoted by David Holmstrom, "We Were a Nomadic People," in *The Christian Science Monitor*, Oct. 19, 1989, 10.
2. "The Filipino people have had the misfortune of being 'liberated' four times during their entire history. First came the Spaniards who 'liberated' them from the 'enslavement to the devil,' next came the Americans who 'liberated' them from their Spanish oppression, then the Japanese who 'liberated' them from American imperialism, then the Americans again who 'liberated' them from the Japanese fascists. After every 'liberation' they found their country occupied by foreign 'benefactors.'" Renato Constantino, *A History of the Philippines: From the Spanish Colonization to the Second World War* (New York and London: Monthly Review Press, 1975), p. 10.
3. The proceedings have been published by the Division of Ordained Ministry of the Board of Higher Education and Ministry, The United Methodist Church. They will be cited hereafter as *Proceedings*, followed by the year and the page number. The quote is from the "Introduction" to *Proceedings*, 1988, p. ix.
4. The "Statement of Purpose" of the Roundtable appears at the end of this book, as Appendix 1.
5. For instance, it was not really Cortez, but his alliance with the Tlaxcaltecans, that defeated the Aztecs. And the history of the so-called Indian wars in North America is well known.
6. These are the materials published in the *Proceedings* already mentioned. The subjects are organized as follows: 1988, hermeneutics and creation; 1989, salvation; 1990, ecclesiology. The list of presenters, and their subjects, appears in Appendix 2.
7. Richard Yaeger, Staff Report, October 20-23, 1988.
8. "Statement of Purpose," in *Proceedings*, 1988, pp. vii-viii.
9. "A Closing Statement," *Ethnic Minority Clergy News*, July 1987, 13.

CHAPTER 2: A VISION OF CATHOLICITY

1. *Adv. haer.* 3.11.8-9 (*ANF*, 1:428-29). In order not to make this quote exceedingly long, a section has been omitted, as shown by the use of ellipsis points. This is a discussion of the particularities of each of the four gospels, relating them to the symbols that have become traditional: a lion, a man, a calf (later an ox), and an eagle.
2. *Ad. Smyr.* 8.2.
3. Among others, by J. B. Lightfoot, *The Apostolic Fathers* (repr., Hildesheim: Georg Olms, 1973), Part II, vol. 2, p. 310 n. 2.

4. *See* Arist., *De plant.* 2.11; Diog. Laert., 2.8 and 7.4 (here given as the title of a work by Zeno the Stoic, *Katholika*); Polybius, 6.5.3 and 7.4.11. Early Christian authors also use the term "catholic" in the sense of "general" or "universal." Justin Martyr, for instance, speaks of a "catholic" resurrection, meaning a universal resurrection (*Dial.* 82). For these and other references, *see* Lightfoot, *Apostolic Fathers*, Part II, vol. 2, p. 310 n. 2.

5. Its first clear use in this latter sense appears in the *Martyrdom of Polycarp*, 16. But the ancient Latin translation of that text, as well as a Greek manuscript found in Moscow, speaks of the "holy" rather than the "catholic" church. Thus, it appears that the reading "catholic" is not the original. Discounting that text, the earliest such usages of the term "catholic" appear in the Muratorian Fragment and in Clement of Alexandria (*Strom.* 7.17).

6. He is convinced, however, that even on the basis of their mutilated canon the heretics can be refuted: "So firm is the ground upon which these Gospels rest, that the very heretics themselves bear witness to them, and, starting from these [documents], each one of them endeavors to establish his own peculiar doctrine. For the Ebionites, who use Matthew's Gospel only, are confuted out of this very same, making false suppositions with regard to the Lord. But Marcion, mutilating that according to Luke, is proved to be a blasphemer of the only existing God, from those [passages] which he still retains. Those, again, who separate Jesus from Christ, alleging that Christ remained impassible, but that it was Jesus who suffered, preferring the Gospel by Mark, if they read it with a love of truth, may have their errors rectified. Those, moreover, who follow Valentinus, making copious use of that according to John, to illustrate their conjunctions, shall be proved to be totally in error by means of this very Gospel, as I have shown in the first book. Since, then, our opponents do bear testimony to us, and make use of these [documents], our proof derived from them is firm and true" (*Adv. haer.* 3.11.7; *ANF* 1:428).

7. *See* my book, *Christian Thought Revisited: Three Types of Theology* (Nashville: Abingdon Press, 1989), where this characteristic of the theology of Irenaeus and of the early church is described in detail.

8. There was a similar dimension of openness in the earliest versions of the doctrine of apostolic succession, which later became a means of excluding all who could not claim a literal, mechanistic succession from the apostles. Originally, this doctrine was developed to oppose those who claimed that they had received a secret doctrine through a private succession from a particular apostle. Over against such claims, the church at large insisted on the open tradition received from *all* the apostles, through *all* their successors, and shared alike by those successors and by all those others who agreed with them.

9. *The Founding of the Church Universal*, vol. 2 of *A History of the Early Church* (London: Lutterworth, 1938), pp. 98-99.

10. Because they understood the authority of Scripture as similar to the authority of a Greek oracle, several among the ancients, both Jew and Christian, decided that if there are two different accounts of creation this must be because there were two different creations. Among the Jews, *see* Philo, *De opif.* 138, *Leg. alleg.* 1.31. Among the Christians, Origen, *De principiis*, 1.3; 2.8. I have discussed this in greater detail in *Christian Thought Revisited*, pp. 42-43.

11. Told by Charles Eastman, and quoted by Vine Deloria, *God Is Red* (New York: Grosset & Dunlap, 1973), p. 99.

12. According to orthodox Moslem tradition, the Koran exists from all eternity, written on a tablet which is kept on the highest heaven. The successive revelations to Mohammed (*suras*) came as Gabriel would bring a portion of the eternal Koran to a lower heaven, to which the Prophet was transported in order to receive dictation. Hearing the words from Gabriel, Mohammed would repeat them, usually to his scribe, Zayd ibn Tabit. Others circulated orally among those who heard and memorized them. All of them, however, have come down directly from heaven, and are a true and exact rendering of the eternal word of God. Even so, Moslem theologians, like the Jewish and Christian counterparts, have had to deal with the apparent contradictions among some of the various *suras*.

13. Lamin Sanneh, *Translating the Message: The Missionary Impact on Culture* (Maryknoll, N.Y.: Orbis Books, 1989), p. 27.

14. "Search for a Theological Paradigm: An Asian-American Journey," *Ethnic Minority Clergy News*, July 1987, 2, 4.
15. Biblical Hermeneutics and the Black Religious Experience," in *Proceedings*, 1988, p. 19.
16. It should be remembered, however, that there have been cases in which the sense of cultural superiority of missionaries was such that they insisted that their converts learn their language. In the United States, there was resistance among some groups to translating the Bible into Native American languages. As Homer Noley, himself a Choctaw, has pointed out, among the Choctaws the word for "God" is lost, because the missionaries thought it was a pagan word, incapable of referring to the God of the Bible. What the Choctaws now use is a corruption of "Jehovah."
17. *Translating the Message*, p. 29.
18. I am consciously using this spelling, "*in*culturation," in order to hint at its parallelism with *in*carnation. According to Webster's *Third New International Dictionary*, "enculturation" is "the process by which an individual learns the traditional content of a culture and assimilates its practices and values." What I mean by "inculturation" is more active and purposeful. It is the process whereby Christianity enters a culture by becoming part of it. Clearly, this involves what Webster's calls "enculturation," but goes beyond it.
19. By "acculturation," I mean the process whereby converts of another culture abandon most or part of their traditional culture and adopt the culture of those from whom they learned the Christian faith.
20. Ernesto Cavassa, "Vivir lo de Dios de otro modo: inculturación y fe," *Páginas* (Lima), 6 (1990), p. 25.
21. On this point, *see* the very able and succinct criticism of such "translation" theories in Robert J. Schreiter, *Constructing Local Theologies* (Maryknoll, N.Y.: Orbis Books, 1985), pp. 6-9.
22. "From I-Hermeneutics to We-Hermeneutics: Prolegomenon to Theology of Community from an Asian-American Perspective," in *Proceedings*, 1988, pp. 47-48.
23. "Theological Impotence and the Universality of the Church," in Gerald H. Anderson and Thomas F. Stransky, eds., *Mission Trends No. 3* (New York and Grand Rapids: Paulist and Eerdmans, 1976), p. 9.
24. Cavassa, "Vivir lo de Dios," p. 20.
25. *Constructing Local Theologies*, p. 29.
26. A phrase taken from Harvey Cox, "Inculturation Reconsidered," *Christianity and Crisis*, May 13, 1991, 141.
27. Ibid., 140.
28. Ibid., 142.
29. "Search for a Theological Paradigm," 4.

CHAPTER 3: VISIONS OF THE WORD

1. *Proceedings*, 1988, pp. 1-6.
2. Peter Marshall, Jr., and David Manuel, *The Light and the Glory* (Old Tappan, N.J.: Fleming H. Revell, 1977).
3. "From I-Hermeneutics to We-Hermeneutics: Prolegomenon to Theology of Community from an Asian-American Perspective," in *Proceedings*, 1988, p. 47.
4. *Proceedings*, 1988, pp. 9-14. This paper is an earlier version of the material found in chapter 5 of a book I published later: *Mañana: Christian Theology from a Hispanic Perspective* (Nashville: Abingdon Press, 1990).
5. "Biblical Hermeneutics and the Black Religious Experience," in *Proceedings*, 1988, pp. 27-34. This material has also been published more recently as part of Dr. Felder's challenging book *Troubling Biblical Waters: Race, Class, and Family* (Maryknoll, N.Y.: Orbis Books, 1989).
6. Among others, Felder makes extensive use of the scholarly dissertation by Cheikh Anta Chiop, *The African Origin of Civilization: Myth or Reality?* Eng. trans. by Mercer Cook (New York and Westport: Lawrence Hill and Co., 1974 [1955]).
7. "Biblical Hermeneutics," p. 21. A point on which respondent James M. Shropshire agreed: "At least one question for Black people becomes: 'Do I identify with the Hebrews who tell the story of being mistreated by Africans or do I identify with the Egyptians from

whom I likely descend as a people and whose story is my story?' The story of faith and the story of cultural heritage may well be seen to confront each other as opposites—especially in a socio-cultural context which has deliberately distorted African history and heritage." It should be added at this point that Felder also argues (p. 22) that the Hebrews leaving Egypt "were themselves most probably a racially mixed stock of people, viz. Afroasiatics."

8. "Biblical Hermeneutics," p. 21.
9. *The Early Versions of the New Testament* (Oxford: Clarendon Press, 1971), p. 216; quoted by Felder, "Biblical Hermeneutics," p. 33 n. 51.
10. "Africa and the Biblical Period," *Harvard Theological Review* 64 (1971) 485.
11. "Biblical Hermeneutics," p. 20.
12. Ibid., p. 29.
13. "Native Americans and the Hermeneutical Task," in *Proceedings*, p. 4.
14. "Hermeneutics: A Hispanic Perspective," p. 9. This is the theme of the "hermeneutics of suspicion," so common in the writings of Latin American and other liberation theologians. I have written more extensively on the subject in Justo L. González and Catherine G. González, *Liberation Preaching: The Pulpit and the Oppressed* (Nashville: Abingdon, 1980), *passim*, but esp. pp. 32-33.
15. "Biblical Hermeneutics," pp. 24-25.
16. One example that corroborates what Felder says is the history of the debate regarding the book of Revelation. The most strenuous objections against its inclusion in the canon came after the time of Constantine, when a book that spoke of Rome as the harlot sitting on seven hills and drunk with the blood of the martyrs became politically objectionable.
17. Dennis R. MacDonald, *The Legend and the Apostle: The Battle for Paul in Story and Canon* (Philadelphia: Westminster Press, 1983).
18. "Native Americans and the Hermeneutical Task," p. 4. In his response, Marvin Abrams agrees: "Response to the Paper Presented by Homer Noley," *Proceedings*, 1988, p. 7.
19. "Biblical Hermeneutics," p. 24.
20. *See*, e.g., Ricci's positive evaluation of God's revelation to the ancient Chinese: *Della entrata della Compagnia di Gesù e Christianità nella Cina*, 1.10.170 in *Fonti Ricciane* (Roma: Libreria dello Stato, 1942), vol. 1, pp. 108-10.
21. "Biblical Hermeneutics," p. 18.
22. *White Women's Christ and Black Women's Jesus: Feminist Christology and Womanist Response* (Atlanta: Scholars Press, 1989), p. 211.
23. The paragraphs that follow, on the Quadrilateral, are an adaptation of part of my summary of the results of the 1987 preliminary meeting of the Roundtable. *See* "A Closing Statement," in *Ethnic Minority Clergy News*, April 1987, 11.
24. Kim, "From I-Hermeneutics," pp. 45-46.
25. "Search for a Theological Paradigm: An Asian-American Journey," *Ethnic Minority Clergy News*, July 1987, 3.
26. In *Mañana*, pp. 120-23, I have claimed and attempted to show that the commonly held understanding of "reason," leading to a view of the universe as a "closed" and mechanistic reality is ideologically determined, and its purpose is to serve the status quo.
27. Several such parallels may be seen in the paper presented by Sione 'Amanake Havea, "Creation and Biblical Faith: Pacific Perspective," in *Proceedings*, 1988, pp. 95-99.
28. *Mañana*, p. 121.
29. "Biblical Hermeneutics," p. 17.
30. Norman K. Gottwald, *The Tribes of Yahweh: A Sociology of the Religion of Liberated Israel 1250–1050 B.C.E.* (Maryknoll, N.Y.: Orbis Books, 1979), p. 10.
31. Lloyd K. Wake, "Salvation, Struggle, and Survival: An Asian-American Reflection," in *Proceedings*, 1989, p. 33.
32. Along these lines, probably the best-known example is Ernesto Cardenal's four-volume collection, *The Gospel in Solentiname* (Maryknoll, N.Y.: Orbis Books, 1976). A group of peasants and fisherfolk on an island gather to read the gospel, and come up with astonishing, yet surprisingly insightful interpretations.

33. "Native Americans and the Hermeneutical Task," p. 4.

34. Ibid., p. 2.

35. "From I-Hermeneutics," p. 47.

36. "Biblical Hermeneutics," p. 26, on the basis of Nienanya Onwu, "The Current State of Biblical Studies in Africa," *The Journal of Religious Thought,* 41, no. 2 (1984-85):35-46.

37. "Fuenteovejuna" is the title of a play by Lope de Vega which shows the solidarity of a town in response to oppression. For the story of Fuenteovejuna and its connection with the theme of community, see *Mañana,* pp. 28-30.

38. Noley, "Native Americans and the Hermeneutical Task," p. 2: "Native American peoples saw the land base as a gift of the Creator and as a spiritual existence itself; it was to be respected and not abused. Europeans saw land as a commodity to be bartered, sold, and exploited for profit."

39. Leviticus 25:23ff.

40. *Proceedings,* 1988, pp. 37-60.

41. "From I-Hermeneutics," p. 49.

42. Ibid., p. 37. Several participants in the Roundtable challenged Dr. Kim on this point, arguing for the value of a cultural "we," or the "we" of ethnic minorities represented at the Roundtable. To subsume all things into a cosmic "we," they argued, is to be left without tools for discernment between oppressor and oppressed, and therefore without tools for ethical decision.

43. Ibid., p. 49.

44. Ibid., p. 45.

45. Ibid., p. 50.

46. Ibid., p. 43.

47. Ibid., p. 44.

48. A clear proof of such privilege, which Kim quotes quite unintentionally and without explicitly relating it to this subject, is the interpretation by William Barclay that "a man is not a Christian if his first concern is pay.... The Christian works for the joy of serving God and his fellow men" (quoted in ibid., p. 44). As if there were not millions of Christians who find it necessary to work at jobs that are meaningless and bemeaning, only for the sake of survival!

49. Ibid., p. 45.

50. Naomi P. F. Southard, "Response to the Paper Presented by Stephen Kim," *Proceedings,* 1988, p. 62.

51. Ibid., p. 63.

52. In a different context, Lloyd K. Wake agreed: "Conformity to community standards and expectations may provide a sense of solidarity and well-being that enables a community to cope with suffering and oppression, but this conformity may not generate assertive and aggressive leadership which will fight to eradicate the causes of suffering and oppression. Asian-Americans experience the tension and struggle of moving from being conformers to being transformers." "Salvation, Struggle, and Survival: An Asian-American Reflection," p. 30.

53. It is for this reason that there is always a tension between literal equivalency translations and those that follow the principle of "dynamic equivalency." This tension has even led some to speak of a "schism" among Bible translators: B. Smilde, "Het schisma der bijbelvertalers," *Kerk en Theologie,* 23 (1972): 135-43. For an example of these two theories of translation, *see* Eugene A. Nida and Charles R. Taber, *The Theory and Practice of Translation* (Leiden: E. J. Brill, 1969), pp. 27-28. Without taking sides on this debate, it is clear that no matter how literal, or how "dynamically equivalent," a translation is always an interpretation.

54. Significantly, both Philo and Origen, quoted earlier as examples of how this understanding of biblical authority led to the notion of double creation, were also Alexandrines.

55. This posed a problem for Judaism in the first centuries of the Christian era, when Christians began using the Septuagint for their own ends and propaganda. Jews responded by producing newer and more accurate Greek translations of the Hebrew Bible. But the legend regarding the origin of the Septuagint made it very difficult to claim that these

newer translations were closer to the Hebrew original—which in fact they were—and therefore should be preferred.

56. H. J. Schroeder, trans., *Canons and Decrees of the Council of Trent* (St. Louis: B. Herder, 1941), p. 18.
57. It is significant that in some such circles *The Living Bible,* which does not even pretend to be a translation, but rather a paraphrase, has gained enormous authority. And it is even more significant that sometimes that authority is bolstered by claims of divine intervention that are reminiscent of the ancient legends about the Septuagint.
58. Ediberto López, "Salvation, Struggle, and Survival: A Latino Approach," in *Proceedings,* 1989, p. 44.

CHAPTER 4: VISIONS OF THE WORLD

1. The first quotation is from his paper, "A Doctrine of Creation in a Hispanic Perspective," in *Proceedings,* 1988, p. 77. The second, from notes on the discussion following.
2. "Response to the Paper Presented by Henry Young," in *Proceedings,* 1988, p. 92.
3. Ibid., p. 93.
4. *Preface to the Latin Writings.*
5. *Lectures on Galatians,* 1535, in *Luther's Works* (St. Louis: Concordia), vol. 26, pp. 399-400.
6. George Tinker and Paul Schultz, *Rivers of Life: Native Spirituality for American Churches* (Minneapolis: Augsburg-Fortress, 1988), pp. 19-20.
7. Ibid., p. 20.
8. Vine Deloria, Jr., *God Is Red* (New York: Grosset & Dunlap, 1973), p. 92. Deloria draws a correct conclusion from this: "The natural world is thereafter considered as corrupted, and it becomes theoretically beyond redemption. Many Christian theologians have attempted to avoid this conclusion, but it appears to have been a central doctrine of the Christian religion during most of the Christian era" (p. 93).
9. Tinker and Schultz, *Rivers of Life,* p. 32.
10. Deloria, *God Is Red,* p. 96.
11. Tinker and Schultz, *Rivers of Life,* p. 21.
12. Quoted by Deloria, *God Is Red,* p. 105.
13. Such is the main thesis of the early chapters of *Christian Thought Revisited* (Nashville: Abingdon Press, 1989).
14. Henry James Young, "Toward a Model of Creation and Afro-American Empowerment," in *Proceedings,* 1988, p. 84.
15. "Search for a Theological Paradigm: An Asian-American Journey," *Ethnic Minority Clergy News,* July 1987, 2-3.
16. "Toward a Model of Creation," p. 83.
17. "Response," p. 91. Note the similarity between what Dr. Wimberly says about a hermeneutical method consisting of "stories interpreting stories," and what was said in the foregoing chapter regarding the manner in which the Bible is its own best interpreter.
18. "Search for a Theological Paradigm," p. 2.
19. "Toward a Model of Creation," p. 84.
20. "A Doctrine of Creation," pp. 77-78.
21. "Creation: A Native American Perspective," in *Proceedings,* p. 66.
22. "Response to the Paper Presented by Sam Wynn," in *Proceedings,* p. 73.
23. Dee Brown, *Bury My Heart at Wounded Knee* (New York: Holt, Rinehart and Winston, 1970), p. 114.
24. Lloyd K. Wake, "Salvation, Struggle, and Survival: An Asian-American Reflection," in *Proceedings,* 1989, p. 30.
25. "A Doctrine of Creation," p. 78.
26. "Toward a Model of Creation," p. 85.
27. As I tried to show in *Faith and Wealth: A History of Early Christian Ideas on the Origin, Significance, and Use of Money* (San Francisco: Harper & Row, 1990).
28. "Toward a Model of Creation," p. 85.

29. "From I-Hermeneutics to We-Hermeneutics: Prolegomenon to Theology of Community from an Asian-American Perspective," in *Proceedings*, 1988, p. 44.
30. "A Doctrine of Creation," p. 79.
31. Ibid.
32. Ibid.

CHAPTER 5: VISIONS OF SALVATION

1. "Salvation, Struggle, and Survival: An Asian-American Reflection," in *Proceedings*, 1989, pp. 33-34.
2. "Salvation, Struggle, and Survival: A Latino Approach," in *Proceedings*, 1989, p. 58.
3. "Salvation, Survival, Struggle: A Native American Reflection," in *Proceedings*, 1989, p. 26.
4. A tightening which also implied less freedom for those who were not in positions of authority. It was partly as a consequence of the struggle against Gnosticism, and the resulting emphasis on authority, organization, and obedience, that women were progressively excluded from positions of leadership in the early church. On this point, *see* Elaine Pagels, *The Gnostic Gospels* (New York: Random House, 1979). As to how this trend led to a conservative interpretation of Paul, not only on women's issues, but also on other social matters, *see* Dennis R. MacDonald, *The Legend and the Apostle: The Battle for Paul in Story and Canon* (Philadelphia: Westminster Press, 1983).
5. In this regard, it is significant that the orthodox anti-Gnostic writers devoted most of their time to describing and attacking Gnostic speculations on the origin and structure of the universe, including the seemingly endless genealogies of "eons," and said very little about the Gnostic promise of salvation. It is in reading some of the newly discovered ancient Gnostic writings that one comes to the realization that the attraction of Gnosticism was not in the speculations the orthodox polemicists so underscored, but rather in their promise of salvation.
6. Ediberto López makes a passing reference to the book of Revelation that may be helpful in this regard: "In chapter 6 of Revelation the author describes the empire, how it conquers and makes warfare. As a product this warfare impoverished humanity. This was followed by famine and pestilence. The heavenly realm responded to all this oppression with wrath" ("Salvation, Struggle, and Survival: A Latino Approach," p. 58). Perhaps no book in the Bible says more about the wrath of God than does the book of Revelation. Yet, that wrath comes out of God's love. It is wrath against those who conquer and make warfare, and against the resulting oppression.
7. "Salvation, Struggle, and Survival: An Asian-American Reflection," p. 32.
8. Ibid., p. 38.
9. Ibid., p. 31.
10. "Salvation, Struggle, and Survival: A Latino Approach," p. 42.
11. Many examples could be given. I have collected dozens of them in *Faith and Wealth* (San Francisco: Harper & Row, 1990), pp. 149-222. Simply to offer a flavor of this preaching, I offer two quotes that appear in that book, one from Basil (p. 176), and the other from Chrysostom (p. 205). From Basil: "When their time comes, seeds germinate and animals grow; but interest begins to reproduce from the moment it is begotten. The beasts become fertile soon, but cease reproducing equally soon. Capital, on the other hand, immediately produces interests, and these continue multiplying into infinity. Everything that grows stops growing when it reaches its normal size. But the money of the greedy never stops growing." From Chrysostom: "Let us not become more beastly than the beasts. For them, all things are common: the earth, the springs, the pastures, the mountains, the valleys. One does not have more than another. You, however, who call yourself human, the tamest of animals, become fiercer than the beasts and shut up in a single house the sustenance for thousands of poor people."
12. Such people would have difficulty with an understanding of salvation such as the one espoused by López himself: "This is not a mythical salvation, nor is it merely catharsis; we are talking about constructing a just and fair society for Latinos in the U.S.A. We recognize that in order for us to be saved from the oppressive structures we are required to enter into a long struggle for political, social, racial, and economic justice in this country" ("Salvation, Struggle, and Survival: A Latino Approach"), p. 46.

13. In his paper, Cain H. Felder quoted James Cone's declaration that "the struggle for justice in this world is not the ultimate goal of faith." "Survival, Struggle, and Salvation: An African-American Theological Reflection," in *Proceedings,* 1989, p. 19, quoting Cone, *For My People: Black Theology and the Black Church* (Maryknoll, N.Y.: Orbis Books, 1984), p. 187.
14. "Salvation, Survival, Struggle: A Native American Reflection," p. 25.
15. "Salvation, Struggle, and Survival: An Asian-American Reflection," pp. 31-32.

CHAPTER 6: VISIONS OF THE CHURCH

1. "Community of Faith: The Sacred Circle of Life," in *Proceedings,* 1990, pp. 70-71.
2. Quoted in Homer Noley, *First White Frost: Native Americans and United Methodism* (Nashville: Abingdon Press, 1991), p. 192.
3. Ibid.
4. "The Church As a Community of Faith," in *Proceedings,* 1990, p. 78.
5. "Lead Us Now to Make New History," in *Proceedings,* 1990, p. 64.
6. "Salvation, Struggle, and Survival: An Asian-American Reflection," in *Proceedings,* 1989, pp. 37-38.
7. "Lead Us Now," p. 65.
8. Jacquelyn Grant lists three of these as central to black women's experience: "Black women must do theology out of their tridimensional experience of racism/sexism/classism. To ignore any aspect of this experience is to deny the holistic and integrated reality of Black womanhood." *White Women's Christ and Black Women's Jesus: Feminist Christology and Womanist Response* (Atlanta: Scholars Press, 1989), p. 209.
9. "Historical Perspective of Latino Ecclesiologies," in *Proceedings,* 1990, p. 85.
10. Ibid., p. 88.
11. "Survival, Struggle, and Salvation: An African-American Theological Reflection," in *Proceedings,* 1989, p. 21.
12. "Community of Faith," p. 70.
13. This contrasts with the wiser attitude of Sitting Bull, quoted in a different context by Abrams: "I have advised my people this way. When you find something good in the white man's road, pick it up. When you find something that is bad, or turns out bad, drop it and leave it alone." Ibid., p. 72.
14. Ibid., p. 69.
15. As far as I know, the first Christian to do so was Tertullian, early in the third century: *De corona,* xi.
16. Murrey Lionel Wax, *Indian American: Unity and Diversity* (Englewood Cliffs, N.J.: Prentice Hall, 1971), pp. 48-49. Quoted by Abrams, "Community of Faith," p. 70.
17. "From I-Hermeneutics to We-Hermeneutics: Prolegomenon to Theology of Community from an Asian-American Perspective," in *Proceedings,* 1988, p. 54.
18. "Survival, Struggle, and Salvation: An African-American Theological Reflection," p. 21.
19. "Historical Perspective," p. 82.
20. "Lead Us Now," p. 63. (Apparently the word "rehearsing," which appeared in the original presentation, has been deleted by the editors.)
21. "Community of Faith," p. 72.
22. "Historical Perspective," pp. 81-86, based on Orlando Costas, *Hacia una teología de la evangelización* (Buenos Aires: La Aurora, 1973).
23. *Apol.* 2.1. The *Apology* has survived in several versions. The division of humankind just quoted appears in the Syriac and Armenian versions. The Greek, which survives only as it was incorporated into the much more recent *Legend of Barlaam and Joasaph,* says that there are Gentiles, Jews, and Christians. For our purpose, the difference between the two versions is immaterial.
24. "Lead Us Now," p. 63.
25. This is my own translation. Unfortunately, the KJV, the RSV, and the NRSV miss the "head" imagery here, in the verb *anakephalaioosasthai.* The NRSV, for instance, says: "to gather up all things in him." In this respect, the Jerusalem Bible is better: "that he would bring everything together under Christ, as head."